Three Guys From Miami
Cook Cuban

Three Guys From Miami

Cook Cuban

Glenn Lindgren,
Raúl Musibay, and Jorge Castillo

Photographs by Nancy Bundt

Gibbs Smith, Publisher
Salt Lake City

First Edition
08 07 06 05 04   5 4 3 2 1

"Three Guys From Miami™" is a trademark of the authors

Published by
Gibbs Smith, Publisher
P.O. Box 667
Layton, Utah 84041

1.800.748.5439 orders
www.gibbs-smith.com

Designed and produced by Reyman Studio
Printed and bound in Hong Kong

Library of Congress Cataloging-in-Publication Data

Lindgren, Glenn M.
Three guys from Miami cook Cuban / by Glenn M. Lindgren, Raúl Musibay,
and Jorge Castillo.—1st ed.
p. cm.
ISBN 1-58685-433-X
1. Cookery, Cuban. I. Musibay, Raúl. II. Castillo, Jorge (Jorge G.) III. Title.
TX716.C8L56 2004
641.597291—dc22
                         2004005051

This book is humbly dedicated
to the people of Cuba in support of their struggles.
It is our fervent hope that the sun will one day rise
on a free and democratic Cuba,
a nation with liberty and human rights for all.

Table of Contents

Seafood 143

Side Dishes 163

Desserts 197

Cuban Food Glossary 215

Sources 224

About the Authors 226

Index 228

Introduction

WELCOME TO OUR first cookbook. If you are one of the more than three million people who have visited our website, iCuban.com: The Internet Cuban, you already know who we are. If you are one of the more than six billion people alive today who have not, a little explanation is in order. We are the Three Guys from Miami—three guys who share a passion for good food, good conversation, and a great party.

We are not classically trained chefs. We have, however, been cooking and eating Cuban food all of our lives—except for Glenn. He's only been cooking and eating it for twenty-three years, but he's working real hard to catch up! Are we experts? We'd certainly like to think so, but how can we be experts when we are learning something new every day? What we can say is that there is no one more dedicated to Cuban food, and we have the waistlines to prove it!

If you are new to Cuban cuisine, you are about to enter a new world of flavor. Cuban cooking combines the tastes of Spain with the tropical flavors of the Caribbean. Throw in some new-world spices and ingredients and a strong African influence and you have the essence of Cuban cookery. Cuban food is highly spiced but NOT spicy hot. Cubans just don't use the hot peppers that are such an integral part of many Latin American cuisines.

Our recipes also reflect, quite naturally, ingredients and methods that were refined by Cuban exiles after they came to the United States. Here they found an abundance of foods that were either very scarce or completely unavailable in Castro's Cuba. Fish and seafood are two examples of foods that were rarely enjoyed in Cuba after 1959. It was also impossible to get real olive oil—an ingredient that gives so many Cuban dishes a distinctive Spanish flavor. Exile in the U.S. also exposed Cubans to ingredients they never saw in Havana. Salmon is very popular with Miami Cubans, for example, but unheard of back home in Cuba.

This cookbook represents three lifetimes of enjoying Cuban food and a long process of creating, collecting, and refining the recipes we present here. These are the Cuban food favorites that we have cooked and eaten in our own homes for many years. Many of our recipes are based on longtime family recipes from several generations of the Musibay and Castillo families. In all cases we present our dishes as they are enjoyed today by Cubans in Miami. Although we have added our own twists over the years, our recipes are rooted in the classic dishes of Cuba. You won't find any "Nuevo Latino" or Pan-Latin recipes here!

Wherever possible we have made these dishes simple to prepare. You don't need to be a professional chef to create any of the recipes in this book. You also won't find a lot of esoteric, hard to find, or expensive ingredients such as truffle shavings, couscous, arugula, or anything in aspic! Best of all, you don't need to be Cuban to cook and enjoy these delicious recipes. If a Swedish guy from Minnesota can cook Cuban food (and he does it very well), you can, too!

We must also acknowledge Nitza Villapol, the "Betty

Crocker of Cuba." We can't agree with her political beliefs, but she did help standardize Cuban recipes for the masses. In the 1950s, every new Cuban bride received a copy of her cookbook. Everyone cooking Cuban food today is indebted to her pioneering efforts in collecting Cuban recipes. In fact, several of the dishes we prepare today have their roots in her early work. Just about every home in Miami has a tattered copy of this Cuban food bible. Raúl's wife, Esther, still uses her copy faithfully.

Finally, we owe a debt of gratitude to the many visitors to our Web site from around the world who have helped us with recipe ideas and suggestions, questions and comments that have inspired us to do better, and complaints when a recipe just didn't turn out like it should have. Their encouragement and appreciation have been our inspiration.

So, thank you so much for purchasing our book! We hope that you and your family enjoy these delicious dishes!

Three Guys From Miami

Glenn Lindgren
Raúl Musibay
Jorge Castillo

August 2004

For more information about Cuban food and culture, visit the authors' website—*iCuban.com*: The Internet Cuban—at *http://www.icuban.com*, or better yet, send them an e-mail at 3guys@icuban.com.

MOJITO
A refreshing rum drink with a hint of lime.

Drinks

Jorge: *The secret to Cuban coffee, or* café Cubano, *is that you must use a finely ground, dark-roasted coffee bean.*

Raúl: *Two brands favored by Cubans are Bustelo and Pilón.*

Jorge: *Bustelo is very popular at restaurants and walk-up windows throughout Miami. Pilón is very popular in Cuban homes, although my mom swears by Café la Llave and won't drink anything else.*

Glenn: *To make Cuban coffee you also need an electric espresso machine. You can get a very nice machine for as little as $50 at your local discount retailer!*

Raúl: *Make sure you add the sugar to the pot* BEFORE *you start brewing—as much as you dare, but Cuban coffee needs to be* SWEET. *A good place to start is three or four teaspoons per batch.*

Café Cubano

Cuban Coffee

. . . .

INGREDIENTS

Serves 2 to 4

- 5 tablespoons (more or less) of Cuban dark-roast coffee espresso ground
- 1 cup (8-ounces) water
- 2 to 4–6 teaspoons sugar (to taste; but remember, it's supposed to be very sweet)

1. Follow the instructions on the espresso machine; each brand is a little different.

2. Fill the coffee chamber as directed by the manufacturer for the desired amount. It's usually about 5 tablespoons of espresso ground coffee, packed tightly, to 1 cup of water—more or less. Add 2 to 4–6 teaspoons of sugar to the pot that the coffee drips into. This creates a dark, intensely flavored, very sweet brew.

Café Cubano is usually served in a small *cafecito* cup, similar to a demitasse. In most homes, the serving size is about 2 ounces. In restaurants you will receive a more generous serving, as much as 4 ounces.

Variations:

Café con Leche

Mix equal parts freshly brewed Cuban coffee and hot (usually steamed) milk.

Café Cortadito

Add 2 tablespoons of milk to freshly brewed Cuban coffee.

CAFÉ CUBANO
The Cuban Coffee Tradition

*M*ANY VISITORS TO *Miami are a little intimidated by the many walk-up windows serving Cuban snacks, sandwiches, and the ever-popular Cuban coffee. For Cubans, sharing a coffee with friends is a social event, a daily ritual, and an act of friendship all rolled into one. Learn a little bit about the traditions of drinking Cuban coffee and you will be quickly welcomed!*

Café Cubano, or just a cafecito, is espresso coffee Cuban-style. It is very strong and sweet; as it brews, the coffee actually drips into a little pot containing several teaspoons of sugar. Once the pot begins to fill, the person making the café uses a spoon to stir up the first few drops of coffee with the sugar in the pot to create a sweet, frothy foam called espumita. *This will rise to the top when the coffee is poured into the cup.*

Cuban coffee is served in a small cup—like a shot of espresso. Step up to the walk-up window, order a café Cubano, or cafecito. You pay when you get it and you'll be surprised at how cheap it is! Most places in Miami sell it for as little as fifty cents! Once your cafecito arrives, you normally drink it at the counter. Don't be surprised if your fellow cafecito drinkers strike up a conversation. A cafecito and conversation go hand in hand!

You can also order Cuban coffee to go. If you order a colada, you'll get a Styrofoam cup with a lid and several small plastic cups so you can share with friends! You'll also notice that most coffee take-out windows provide cold water and paper cups. Some people drink the cold water first to clear the palate; others drink it last to dilute the coffee in the stomach—it's a topic of much debate.

For many non-Cubans, it takes a while to develop a taste for Cuban coffee. If you need to get used to the taste, try ordering a cortadito, which has milk added—anywhere from one or two tablespoons to half milk and half coffee.

The last way to drink Cuban coffee is in a café con leche. In most places you get a small cup of hot milk and a shot of Cuban coffee in a demitasse cup. At the table or counter, you dump the coffee into the milk and stir with a spoon. Café con leche is usually a breakfast drink, and you dunk Cuban bread or pastries into it. The next time you're in Miami, step up to the counter and order a cafecito!

Raúl: *Cuba libre is Spanish for "Free Cuba." Unfortunately under Castro, the name of this drink has become a joke. There is no freedom in Cuba today. If you drink one, it's a nice gesture to make a toast: "Here's to a* FREE *and democratic Cuba!"*

Jorge: *If you're drinking one in a Miami bar, just shout out* que viva Cuba libre *(long live a free Cuba). You might be surprised to find that someone in the bar has bought your next round.*

Cuba Libre
Rum and Coke

. . . .

INGREDIENTS

Serves 1

1½   ounces white rum

6   ounces ice cold Coca-Cola

Juice of ½ lime

Ice cubes

Lime twist

1. Pour rum in a tall glass. Fill with cold Coke, add a squeeze of lime juice, and stir. Add ice and garnish with a twist of lime.

4

Mojito

Rum Drink

. . . .

INGREDIENTS

Serves 1

3   teaspoons sugar

Juice of ½ lime

Fresh yerba buena (or mint) leaves

1   ounce white rum

Ice cubes

Soda water

1. Put sugar and lime juice in a glass. Crush a few fresh mint leaves into the sugar and lime juice. Add rum and ice cubes. Fill with soda water and serve with a sprig of mint.

Raúl: *The* mojito *is a classic drink in Cuba. It got its origin in the cane fields, where workers were provided with large barrels of sugarcane juice, what we call* guarapo, *to drink after a hot day cutting sugarcane.*

Glenn: *On Saturday nights, the plantation owners would spike the* guarapo *with a little* aguardiente, *a crude form of rum; thus began a long tradition of Saturday night Cuban parties!*

Jorge: *As time went on, the workers began adding* yerba buena, *a type of mint leaf, to the barrel for flavor. Today the best* mojitos *are sill made with this leaf. If you have a Latin market in your neighborhood, you might be able to find some. It has to be fresh!*

Glenn: *If not, use spearmint or peppermint—again fresh from the garden. They are the best substitutes.*

Jorge: *We've noticed lately that some trendy restaurants and bars have been serving a very dry* mojito. *The classic* mojito *should be very sweet!*

Raúl: Mojitos *are really delicious and refreshing on a hot August day in Miami!*

. . . .

GUARAPO

*G**UARAPO IS FRESH** sugarcane juice. It has a very light flavor (*NOT *super sweet like many people assume) and is extremely refreshing on a hot day. In fact, the sugar content of* guarapo *makes it just slightly sweeter than orange juice. Guarapo is really quite healthy and works better than Gatorade to get into your system quickly! Much of the* guarapo *sold in Miami is made from sugarcane grown in western Palm Beach County, southeast of Lake Okeechobee. The sweetest and most flavorful* guarapo *is available in winter when there is not as much rain.*

Ponche Habana Para Los Niños

Havana Punch for Kids

. . . .

INGREDIENTS

Serves 16

1	cup water
¼	cup honey
¼	cup sugar
2	cinnamon sticks
4	whole cloves
1½	cups fresh pineapple juice (or from frozen concentrate)
2	cups fresh orange juice (or from frozen concentrate)
¼	cup fresh lime juice
1	quart lemon sherbet (softened for about 20 to 30 minutes at room temperature)
2	cans ice cold ginger ale

Jorge: *Kids are a big part of every Cuban celebration.*

Raúl: *Our families are very important to us, and everybody is included.*

Glenn: *While the adults tend to drink adult-type beverages, the kids like to drink soft drinks and, on special occasions, delicious tropical fruit punches.*

Raúl: *This delicious punch recipe includes lemon sherbet, which gives it a real kick.*

Jorge: *Why not make a big batch for your next Cuban party? Your kids will love you for it!*

Glenn: *You may even discover you have a Cuban kid or two you never knew about!*

1. To make the syrup, bring water to boiling in a 1-quart saucepan; stir in honey and sugar. Add cinnamon sticks and cloves, stirring thoroughly. Reduce heat to medium low and cook for about 15 to 20 minutes, uncovered, until slightly thickened.

2. Remove syrup from heat and let cool to room temperature. Remove the cinnamon sticks and the whole cloves and place in refrigerator to chill.

3. To make the punch, put the juices and the softened sherbet in a large punch bowl and stir together. Add the spiced syrup and ginger ale. Serve immediately over ice.

Papa Hemingway Daiquiri

. . . .

INGREDIENTS

Serves 1

- 3 ounces grapefruit juice
- 2 ounces white rum
- Splash of maraschino cherry juice or Grenadine
- Crushed ice
- Lime twist

1. Blend grapefruit juice, rum, and maraschino cherry juice. Serve over crushed ice with a lime twist.

Raúl: *Ernest Hemingway loved Cuba and the great fishing to be had along the Cuban coast.*

Jorge: *One of his favorite hangouts was the Floridita in Havana. His favorite drink? The daiquiri.*

Glenn: *Hemingway became convinced that he had diabetes, so he invented a daiquiri without sugar but with twice as much rum!*

Jorge: *The drink became known by various names, including the Hemingway Special or the Papa Hemingway. If you walked into the Floridita today and wanted this drink, you would ask for a "Papa Doble."*

Glenn: *Hemingway used to bring a thermos bottle to the Floridita so that he could transport one of these delicious drinks to enjoy at home.*

Raúl: *He called it a* trago del camino (*literally, drink of the road*).

Glenn: *Thus creating the popular expression "one for the road."*

THE CITY BEAUTIFUL
Grand arches highlight the grounds of the Biltmore Hotel, Coral Gables.

EMPANADAS
Savory Cuban pastries are
good at any meal!

Appetizers

Glenn: *Many Florida Cubans fondly remember picking up a brown paper bag of freshly made* bollitos *from a local bar or small "mom and pop" Cuban restaurant.*

Raúl: Bollitos *are similar to hush puppies, which are served in many Deep South restaurants.*

Jorge: *Except that* bollitos *are made with ground black-eyed peas instead of cornmeal.*

Raúl: *And they taste a lot better!*

Bollitos

. . . .

INGREDIENTS

Serves 4 to 6

2   (15.8-ounce) cans black-eyed peas

5   cloves garlic

1   teaspoon salt

2   teaspoons ground cumin

1   cup finely chopped onion

1   cup seeded and finely chopped green bell pepper

   Olive oil for sautéing

2   tablespoons fresh lime juice

   Vegetable or peanut oil for deep frying

½   cup flour (approximately)

1. Drain all liquid from the canned beans, rinse thoroughly with cold water, and drain again.

2. Grind the peas with the garlic and a little bit of water in a blender until you have a thick, lumpy puree. Add the salt and cumin and blend thoroughly.

3. In a sauté pan, lightly sauté the chopped onion and pepper for 1 or 2 minutes in 2 tablespoons of olive oil. Let cool. In a large bowl, mix the cooked onions and pepper into the ground pea mixture. Add fresh lime juice. Gradually blend in white flour, a little at a time, until your dough is the consistency of cookie dough.

4. Get a large, deep frying pan or saucepan and add vegetable oil to a depth of about three inches. Heat the oil to the frying stage—about 360 to 375 degrees F. Don't let your oil get too hot! You may also use a deep fat fryer if you have one, following all manufacturer's instructions.

5. Drop by tablespoonfuls into the hot oil. (Cook a few at a time and don't overcrowd the pan!) Let them cook until golden brown, turning occasionally—about 3 to 4 minutes.

6. Remove from oil and drain on paper towels. Serve hot with lime wedges and hot sauce if desired.

CLASSIC CADDY
This convertible is at home on the streets of Havanna or Miami.

GARLIC

*W*E HAVE A *little confession to make: we* LOVE *garlic. There are very few dishes that can't be improved by the addition of this pungent bulb! The Egyptians actually worshiped garlic, and although we're not quite that fanatical, we do use a lot of garlic in many of our dishes.*

Garlic is our friend, and we want garlic to be your friend, too! However, if you grew up in a garlic-deprived environment and find yourself to be a little "garlic-a-phobic," by all means cut back on the garlic if you must. But please promise to gradually add the garlic back into these recipes as you develop a taste for Cuban food. You won't regret it!

Glenn: *It's no secret that we love* croquetas! *We could easily eat* croquetas *every day.*

Raúl: Croquetas *are very popular in restaurants, walk-up counters, and bakeries all over Miami. They make a good lunch or snack. Many people even eat them for breakfast!*

Jorge: *Ham is the most popular, although you occasionally see chicken* croquetas *as well.*

Glenn: *Many people bake their* croquetas, *but take it from us, the best ones are fried.*

Jorge: *A good* croqueta *has a crispy shell and a moist middle. They are best when served immediately!*

Raúl: *Hey, eat them fresh and hot or don't bother eating them at all!*

Croquetas de Jamón
Ham Croquettes
. . . .

INGREDIENTS

Serves 6 to 8 (2 croquetas per person)

4	tablespoons butter
1	cup finely minced onion
⅓	cup flour
1½	cups milk (more or less), room temperature
¼	teaspoon nutmeg
1	tablespoon dry sherry
1	tablespoon finely chopped parsley
4	cups (about 1 pound) ground smoked ham
1	cup (more or less) dry bread crumbs
	Salt and black pepper to taste
2	eggs beaten with 1 tablespoon water
1	cup dry bread crumbs mixed with ¼ cup flour
½	teaspoon salt
½	teaspoon pepper
	Vegetable oil for frying

1. Melt the butter in a 3-quart saucepan; add the onions and sauté on medium-low heat until translucent.

2. Gradually whisk in flour to make a roux—add more butter if necessary to make it smooth. Gradually whisk in the milk to form a smooth sauce. Continue cooking until the sauce thickens. Your sauce needs to be very thick—like wallpaper paste! Whisk in nutmeg, sherry, and parsley. Fold in the ground ham and bread crumbs. Let simmer for 5 minutes on low heat, stirring constantly. Taste and season with pepper and a little salt if necessary: the ham probably has enough salt already. Spoon the mixture into a baking dish and refrigerate until well chilled—at least 1 hour.

TIP: The mixture needs to be firm enough to form into rolls. If your mixture is too soft or sticky, add more bread crumbs.

3. Beat the eggs with water in a mixing bowl until frothy. Combine the bread crumbs and flour in a second bowl with salt and pepper. Shape the ham mixture into logs about ¾ inch thick and 3 inches long. Dip the logs in the egg wash and roll the logs in the seasoned bread crumbs. Dip a second time and re-roll in bread crumbs.

IMPORTANT: Cover logs with plastic wrap and refrigerate for 2 to 3 hours. (You may also freeze for later use, or use the freezer to quickly chill them.)

4. In a large frying pan, add enough vegetable oil to cover half the croqueta at a time. Heat the oil to the frying stage—about 360 to 375 degrees F. Sauté a few croquetas at a time in the hot oil for 3 to 4 minutes, turning occasionally, until golden brown. Remove from oil and drain on paper towels.

Immediately make loud noises, pretend someone is at the door, or otherwise endeavor to distract any bystanders. This will prevent the hungry from attacking the croquetas before they are cool enough to eat safely! Believe us, fresh croquetas have a habit of rapidly and mysteriously disappearing!

CILANTRO

Over the years, some people have asked us about the use of cilantro in so many of our recipes. "Isn't cilantro a spice used in Mexican food, not Cuban?" or "When I left Cuba in 1960, nobody was using cilantro in their cooking." We obviously can't speak for every Cuban in Cuba, but both Jorge and Raúl's family grew their own cilantro (and its cousin culantro) in their backyards in Cuba going back several decades before Castro. In fact, culantro grows wild all over Cuba.

Visit any Miami grocery and you will see both of these herbs sold in abundance. So, yes, cilantro is an "authentic" Cuban ingredient! Besides, it just tastes great in so many dishes!

Glenn: *This great version of* croquetas *combines the taste of ham with mashed potatoes.*

Jorge: *They taste a little like a papa rellena made with a ham filling except in this case the ham is blended with the potatoes …*

Raúl: *… like a Cuban tamal. I love them!*

Croquetas de Papas y Jamón
Potato and Ham Croquettes

· ·

INGREDIENTS

Serves 6 to 8 (2 croquetas per person)

4 tablespoons butter

1 cup finely minced onion

1 tablespoon dry sherry

1 tablespoon finely chopped fresh chives

4 cups ground smoked ham

3 cups cooked mashed potatoes

Salt and pepper to taste

2 eggs beaten with 1 tablespoon water

1 cup dry bread crumbs mixed with ¼ cup flour

1 teaspoon salt

½ teaspoon pepper

Vegetable oil for frying

16

1. Melt the butter in a 3-quart saucepan; add the onions and sauté on medium-low heat until translucent. Whisk in sherry and chives. Add ground ham. Let simmer for 5 minutes on low heat. Remove from heat, add mashed potatoes and blend completely. Taste and season with pepper and a little salt if necessary. The ham probably has enough salt already. Spoon the mixture into a baking dish and refrigerate until well chilled, at least 1 hour.

TIP: The mixture needs to be firm enough to form into rolls. If the mixture is too soft or sticky, mix in some bread crumbs.

2. Beat the eggs with water in a mixing bowl until frothy. Combine the bread crumbs and flour in a second bowl with salt and pepper. Shape the ham/potato mixture into logs about ¾ inch thick and 3 inches long. Dip the logs in the egg wash and roll them in the seasoned bread crumbs. Dip a second time and roll again in bread crumbs until they are completely covered.

IMPORTANT: Place the logs in a lightly greased baking dish, cover with plastic wrap, and refrigerate for 2 to 3 hours. (You may also freeze for later use, or use the freezer to quickly chill them.)

3. In a large frying pan, add enough vegetable oil to cover half the croqueta at a time. Heat the oil to the frying stage—about 360 to 375 degrees F. Sauté a few croquetas at a time in the hot oil for 3 to 4 minutes, turning occasionally, until golden brown. Remove from oil and drain on paper towels.

Glenn: *In Spanish, empanar means "to bread," or coat with bread crumbs. Empanadas are pastries filled with meat, seafood, cheese, and so on. Although this dish probably originated in Galicia in Spain, it is now a common dish throughout Latin America.*

Jorge: *Empanadas are extremely popular in Argentina, and many of the Argentine varieties include hard-boiled eggs and raisins!*

Raúl: *Empanadas are a popular item for street vendors because these pastries are easy to eat on the run.*

Jorge: *Empanadas come in all sizes, from large "complete meal" versions to small little bocaditos, used as appetizers at parties and family gatherings.*

Glenn: *In Cuba, the empanada was most likely introduced by the Spanish and given an island flavor with a touch of citrus, garlic, onion, and pepper.*

Empanadas
Cuban Pastries

. . . .

Empanadas: Baked Dough Recipe

INGREDIENTS

Serves 4 to 8 (makes 6 to 8 medium empanadas)

1½	cups all-purpose flour
½	teaspoon salt
1	teaspoon baking powder
1	tablespoon sugar
8	ounces cream cheese, softened
1	stick butter, softened
1	large egg beaten lightly with ¼ teaspoon water

1. Sift the flour, then sift it again with the salt, baking powder, and sugar, and set aside. In a large bowl, use an electric or stand mixer to mix the cream cheese and butter together until well blended. Gradually add the flour mixture and mix until smooth. Place the dough in a bowl, cover and refrigerate at least 30 minutes.

2. Preheat the oven to 350 degrees F.

3. Prepare the filling according to one of the empanada recipes on the following pages.

4. Lightly flour a work surface. Divide the dough into 4 pieces (keep the pieces you aren't using in the refrigerator until you need them); use a floured rolling pin to roll out the dough to about ⅛ inch thick. Cut the dough into a large, rough circle. (Don't worry about making a perfect circle. You will trim the dough in the following steps.) Put some filling in the center of the circle and fold over to make a half circle. Don't over-fill! Use a pizza wheel to trim away the excess dough and make a nice half-moon shape. Seal the edges of the dough with your fingers to make a scalloped edge.

5. Place the pastries 2 inches apart on a lightly greased cookie sheet, brush with the egg wash, and bake until lightly browned, 15 to 20 minutes. They also can be made ahead of time, refrigerated, and reheated in a 350-degree oven for 4 to 6 minutes.

Empanadas
Cuban Pastries

. . . .

Empanadas: Fried Dough Recipe

INGREDIENTS

Serves 4 to 8 (makes 6 to 8 medium empanadas)

2	cups flour
½	teaspoon salt
1	teaspoon baking powder
1	teaspoon sugar
4	tablespoons lard
2	tablespoons butter
1	whole egg + 1 egg yolk
½	cup cold water (more or less, to bring dough to proper consistency)

1. Sift the flour with salt, baking powder, and sugar. Place half of the flour in a large mixing bowl. Make a well in the center. Place the lard, butter, eggs, and water in the well. Use an electric or stand mixer to mix ingredients into a paste. Continue to mix, gradually adding more flour until all of the flour is added. You may need to add water—slowly and in small quantities—until the dough reaches a soft, pliable consistency, like pie dough. Place the dough in a bowl, cover and refrigerate at least 30 minutes.

2. Prepare the filling according to one of the empanada recipes on the following pages.

3. Lightly flour a work surface. Divide the dough into 4 pieces (keep the pieces you aren't using in the refrigerator until you need them); use a floured rolling pin to roll out the dough about 1/8 inch thick. Cut the dough into a large, rough circle. (Don't worry about making a perfect circle. You will trim the dough in the following steps.) Put some filling in the center of the circle and fold over to make a half circle. Don't over-fill! Use a pizza wheel to trim away the excess dough and make a nice half-moon shape. Seal the edges of the dough with your fingers to make a scalloped edge.

Instructions for pan frying:

In a large frying pan, add enough vegetable oil to cover the empanadas completely. Heat the oil to the frying stage, about 360 to 375 degrees F. Fry the empanadas in the oil, turning occasionally until brown on all sides. Drain on paper towels and serve hot!

Instructions for deep-fat frying:

Heat the oil to 375 degrees F. Place a single layer of empanadas in the fryer basket, drop in hot oil, and cook for approximately 2 to 3 minutes, until golden brown. Be careful not to overcook. Follow the manufacturer's instructions for your deep fat fryer. Drain on paper towels and serve hot!

Empanadas de Pollo
Chicken Empanadas

· ·

INGREDIENTS

1	cup finely chopped onion
3	tablespoons olive oil
3	cloves garlic, minced
4	chicken thighs, skin-on, bone-in
1	bay leaf
1	cup chicken broth
¼	cup white wine
½	teaspoon salt
¼	teaspoon pepper
3	tablespoons flour
3	tablespoons cornstarch mixed with ¼ cup water

1. Sauté the onion over medium heat in 2 tablespoons olive oil for 2 to 3 minutes, or until translucent. Add garlic and cook an additional minute, stirring constantly. Remove from heat and set aside.

2. Place chicken, bay leaf, chicken broth, wine, salt, and pepper in a 3-quart saucepan. Add enough water to just cover the chicken. Bring to a boil, reduce heat to low, and simmer until the chicken is cooked, about 30 minutes. Remove the chicken and allow it to cool. Strain and save the broth.

3. When the chicken is cool enough to handle, skin and de-bone. Finely shred the meat. Place the cooked chicken in a 3-quart saucepan with 1 tablespoon olive oil. Stir in the onion/garlic mixture, and gradually add the flour. Stir in ¼ cup of the broth. Bring to a boil, reduce heat to low and simmer for 5 to 10 minutes. Use enough cornstarch mixed with water to make the filling thick and moist, but not runny. Put some filling in the center of each circle of dough, trim away excess dough, seal, and cook as indicated in the baked (page 18) or fried (page 20) recipe.

Empanadas de Pollo y Queso
Chicken and Cheese Empanadas

. . . .

INGREDIENTS

1	cup grated mild white cheese
1	cup cooked and shredded chicken dark meat
2	cloves garlic, minced
2	green onions, minced
½	teaspoon ground cumin
1	tablespoon fresh lime juice
	Salt and pepper to taste

1. Mix all ingredients in a bowl, taste and adjust the seasonings as necessary. Keep refrigerated until empanadas are ready to be stuffed. Put some of the filling in the center of each circle of dough, then seal and cook as indicated in the baked (page 18) or fried (page 20) recipe.

Empanadas de Camarones

Shrimp Empanadas

. . . .

INGREDIENTS

1	cup finely chopped white onion
3	tablespoons olive oil
¾	pound raw medium shrimp (36 to 40 count per pound), peeled and deveined
3	cloves garlic, mashed
2	cups peeled and finely chopped Roma tomatoes
¼	teaspoon ground cumin
¼	teaspoon white pepper
1	teaspoon salt
¼	cup chopped fresh cilantro

1. Sauté the onion over medium heat in the olive oil for 2 to 3 minutes, or until translucent. Add raw shrimp as suggested above. (You don't need any bigger than medium and you'll save money with the smaller size.) Add garlic, shrimp, tomatoes, cumin, pepper, and salt, stirring lightly. Cook an additional 2 minutes only, stirring constantly until the shrimp just start turning pink. Set filling aside and let cool.

2. Put some of the filling in the center of each circle of dough, and sprinkle with a little fresh cilantro. Trim away excess dough, seal, and cook as indicated in the baked or fried recipe. If you have any leftover filling, don't despair! It tastes great on Cuban toast!

Empanadas de Carne Asada

Beef Empanadas

. . . .

INGREDIENTS

1	cup finely chopped onion
1	cup chopped green pepper
2	tablespoons olive oil
3	cloves garlic, minced
¼	teaspoon cinnamon
½	teaspoon oregano
	Salt and black pepper to taste
1	pound leftover beef roast, shredded

1. Prepare a sofrito by sautéing the onion and green pepper over medium heat in the olive oil for 2 or 3 minutes, or until translucent. Add garlic and cook an additional minute, stirring constantly.

2. Add cinnamon, oregano, and roast beef, and cook until heated through. Salt and pepper the mixture to taste. Put some of the filling in the center of each circle of dough, trim away excess dough, seal, and cook as indicated in the baked (page 18) or fried recipe (page 20).

SOFRITO

A SOFRITO *IS that unique combination of green pepper, onions, garlic, tomato (sometimes), and spices that is at the heart of so many great Cuban dishes. Many people like to use a pre-made* sofrito, *either one that they make themselves or one that is commercially prepared. In a pinch, a little pre-made* sofrito *can really spice up a simple stew, soup, or rice dish. However, we believe you create the best flavors when you make the* sofrito *fresh as part of the preparation of each dish. So, when we tell you to sauté peppers, onion, and garlic, we are really asking you to "prepare a sofrito."*

Empandas de Cangrejo
Crab Empanadas

. . . .

INGREDIENTS

1½	cups red bell pepper, diced
1½	cups green bell pepper, diced
¼	cup diced onion
	Olive oil for sautéing
2	garlic cloves, minced
¾	pound crabmeat
	Salt and pepper to taste
2	eggs
1	tablespoon dry sherry
½	cup bread crumbs

1. Sauté the red and green bell peppers and onions in olive oil until the onions are limp. Add the garlic and sauté for an additional 2 minutes, stirring occasionally. Remove from heat, add crabmeat, and mix thoroughly. Salt and pepper to taste. Let this mixture cool.

2. Beat eggs until frothy. Fold them into the crab mixture. Add dry sherry. Gradually and gently fold in the bread crumbs until the filling is stiff yet pliable. Put some of the filling in the center of each circle of dough, then seal and cook as indicated in the baked (page 18) or fried (page 20) recipe .

Empanadas de Jamón or Chorizo
Ham or Sausage Empanadas

. . . .

INGREDIENTS

6	tablespoons butter
1/4	cup flour
2	cups milk, room temperature
1/4	teaspoon black pepper
1/4	teaspoon nutmeg
2	cups ground ham or ground chorizo

1. Melt the butter in a 3-quart saucepan and make a roux by gradually whisking in the flour until you have a smooth paste. Whisk in the milk and continue cooking on low heat, stirring constantly, until the sauce thickens. Add the pepper and nutmeg. Gradually fold in the ground ham or ground chorizo. The filling should be stiff. Add salt only if necessary after tasting! Put some of the filling in the center of each circle of dough, then seal and cook as indicated on page 18 or 20.

Empanadas de Carne y Cebolla
Beef and Onion Empanadas

. . . .

INGREDIENTS

Olive oil for sautéing

1   pound sirloin steak, cut into ¼ inch cubes

1   cup diced onion

3   cloves garlic, minced

2   tablespoons flour

¼   teaspoon cinnamon

2   tablespoons dry sherry

1   tablespoon sweet Spanish paprika

2   or 3 dashes Tabasco sauce

1   tablespoon chopped fresh parsley

1. In a large sauté pan, sauté the steak, onion, and garlic over medium-high heat. Stir in flour and continue stirring until the onions are limp and the beef is browned. Stir in cinnamon, sherry, paprika, Tabasco sauce, and chopped parsley. Remove from heat, let cool and use to fill empanadas. Put some of the filling in the center of each circle of dough, trim away excess dough, seal, and cook as indicated in the baked (page 18) or fried (page 20) recipe.

Three Guys quench their
thirst with fresh coconut
juice on South Beach.

Glenn: *Hey, Raúl, did you ever have any focaccia in Cuba?*

Raúl: *No way! I never heard of it!*

Jorge: *Well, a while back we needed something original to bring to a party!*

Glenn: *Everybody was expecting something special from the "Three Guys From Miami."*

Jorge: *We experimented a bit in the kitchen, and we got the idea from the Italian focaccia.*

Glenn: *It didn't take us long to figure out how to "Cubanize" it. The key is the fresh cilantro and lime juice.*

Jorge: *Even though this isn't a "traditional" Cuban recipe, it's still a nice appetizer for your next party!*

Focaccia Cubana
Cuban Focaccia

. . . .

INGREDIENTS

Serves 6 to 8

1	tablespoon sugar
1	cup warm water (110 degrees)
2	tablespoons olive oil
1	package yeast
2½ to 3¼	cups white flour
1	teaspoon salt
2 to 4	tablespoons olive oil
2	teaspoons garlic powder (approximately)
¼ to ½	cup chopped fresh cilantro
4 to 6	ripe Roma tomatoes, thinly sliced
	Fresh lime juice
	Salt and freshly ground black pepper to taste
½	cup grated Parmesan cheese

1. Dissolve the sugar and yeast in the water in a small bowl and whisk in the olive oil. Let stand for 10 minutes in a warm place—it should begin to foam.

2. Sift together the flour and the salt. Place the yeast/oil/water mixture in the bowl of a stand mixer with the dough hook attached. Turn the mixer to low and add the flour a little at a time until you have a stiff but pliable dough. Adjust the amount of flour, more or less, to achieve the right consistency. Let the machine knead the dough 2 minutes. Place this smooth ball of dough into a greased bowl; cover, and set aside in a warm place to rise until double in size, about 45 minutes to 1 hour.

3. Preheat the oven to 400 degrees F.

4. Punch down the dough. Remove it from the bowl and place on a lightly oiled, deep-dish pizza pan. Spread the dough out onto the pan. Using your fingertips, make "dimples" in the dough. Prebake the crust for about 10 minutes, and then remove from oven.

5. Liberally drizzle the dough with olive oil, sprinkle on the garlic and cilantro, and spread the tomato slices evenly on the top of the dough. Use enough tomatoes to completely cover the top of the dough. Drizzle lime juice and more olive oil on the tomato slices and lightly shake salt and pepper, by eye, over the top. Add a little more cilantro to the tomato slices for color. Sprinkle with grated Parmesan cheese and bake for an additional 5 to 10 minutes, until the tomatoes sizzle and the cheese starts to brown slightly.

Jorge: *Cubans love* frituras *and they make them with many different ingredients.*

Raúl: *The ones we like best are made with* malanga, *a type of root vegetable that's common in the Caribbean.*

Glenn: *I didn't want to mention this here with my two brothers-in-law listening in, but* malanga *is not really a root vegetable. It's actually a "corm," a compressed underground stem!*

Raúl: *A corm?! What in the heck is that?*

Jorge: *Frituras are a lot like French fries. They need to be cooked and eaten immediately, while they are hot and crisp.*

Glenn: *Make these and you can tell everyone on your block that you had your daily serving of corm, a compressed underground stem!*

Frituras de Malanga
Malanga Fritters

. . . .

INGREDIENTS

Serves 6

3	medium malangas, raw
2	eggs
2	cloves of garlic, mashed
½	teaspoon salt
1	teaspoon lime juice
2	tablespoons parsley, finely chopped
	Vegetable oil for frying

1. Peel the malangas completely. Using a grater, grate the malangas to a medium-fine consistency.

2. Beat the eggs until foamy. Add the garlic, salt, lime juice, and parsley, and mix well. Mix the grated malanga into the mixture with a fork to form a thick paste. Refrigerate mixture for 1 hour.

3. In a large frying pan, add enough vegetable oil to completely cover the frituras. Heat the oil to the frying stage, approximately 360 to 375 degrees F. Carefully drop the fritura mixture into the hot oil by tablespoons. (Watch out for spattering!) Fry approximately 2 to 3 minutes, flipping occasionally, until the frituras are golden brown. Drain on paper towels. Serve immediately!

Always an abundance of
fresh tropical fruit in Little
Havanna, Miami!

Glenn: *Although Cubans do eat potato chips occasionally, plantain and yuca chips are much more popular.*

Raúl: *Oh, man! Go into any supermarket and you will see bags and bags of plantain and yuca chips!*

Glenn: *However, the best chips are prepared fresh and served hot at walk-up windows and cafes.*

Jorge: *Better yet, just follow this recipe and make them at home for a delicious treat!*

Glenn: *These are great when served with Mariquitas Salsa (page 38).*

Mariquitas
Chips

. . . .

Plantain Chips

INGREDIENTS

Serves 2 to 4

2   large green plantains, peeled
Corn or vegetable oil (not olive oil) for frying

1. Cut the plantain into long thin strips with a sharp knife, plantain slicer, or mandolin—the thinner the better.

Instructions for pan frying:

In a large frying pan, add enough vegetable oil to cover the plantain chips completely. Heat the oil to the frying stage, about 360 to 375 degrees F. Fry the plantain chips in the hot oil, turning occasionally, until brown on both sides. Drain on paper towels; keep warm in oven until ready to serve.

Instructions for deep-fat frying:

Heat the oil to 375 degrees F. Place a single layer of plantain chips in the fryer basket, drop into hot oil and cook for approximately 2 to 3 minutes, or until golden brown. Be careful not to overcook. Follow the manufacturer's instructions for your deep fat fryer. Drain on paper towels; keep warm in oven until ready to serve.

36

Yuca Chips

INGREDIENTS

Serves 2 to 4

2   yuca, peeled and cut in half horizontally

Corn or vegetable oil (not olive oil) for deep-fat or
frying-pan frying

1. Cover yuca with water by about 2 inches in a 3-quart saucepan. Bring to a boil, reduce heat to low, and cook, uncovered, until yuca becomes tender but NOT mushy, about 15 minutes or less. Remove yuca and drain thoroughly. Let cool.

2. Cut the cooked yuca into long thin strips with a sharp knife, plantain slicer, or mandolin—the thinner the better.

Instructions for pan frying:

In a large frying pan, add enough vegetable oil to cover the yuca chips completely. Heat the oil to the frying stage, about 360 to 375 degrees F. Fry the yuca chips in the hot oil, turning occasionally until brown on both sides. Drain on paper towels; keep warm in oven until ready to serve.

Instructions for deep-fat frying:

Heat the oil to 375 degrees F. Place a single layer of yuca chips in the fryer basket, drop into hot oil, and cook for approximately 2 to 3 minutes, or until golden brown. Be careful not to overcook. Follow the manufacturer's instructions for your deep fat fryer. Drain on paper towels; keep warm in oven until ready to serve.

Raúl: *This is the sauce they serve at Miami restaurants.*

Glenn: *It's a very garlicky, sour sauce that tastes great on a hot fresh chip!*

Jorge: *Once you've had chips this way, you'll never want to eat a plain chip again!*

Glenn: *And best of all, with all of that garlic this one is guaranteed to keep vampires and insurance sales people from getting too close to you!*

Mariquitas Salsa
Sauce for Chips

. . . .

INGREDIENTS

8	cloves of garlic
¼	cup chopped fresh cilantro leaves
	Juice of 1 lime
2	tablespoons white vinegar
½	cup olive oil
	Salt and pepper to taste

1. Place the garlic, cilantro leaves, lime juice, and white vinegar in a food processor and puree until thoroughly chopped.

2. Heat the olive oil in a small saucepan until hot but not smoking. Remove pan from heat. Pour the pureed garlic-and-cilantro mixture into the hot oil, whisking constantly for 1 or 2 minutes.

3. Serve warm. The sauce should have an intense garlic/sour flavor. Use a fresh, hot mariquita to test!

PALMS AND ARCHITECTURE
There is nothing like a drive
through Coral Gables on a
Sunday afternoon.

Raúl: *This is one Cuban snack that if you haven't tried, you probably don't know what in the heck it is.*

Jorge: *When we have guests from out of town, we ask them if they'd like to try one and they almost always ask, "What in the heck is that?"*

Glenn: *Even if you try to explain it . . .*

Jorge: *. . . they just don't get it!*

Glenn: *So the best way is not to say anything at all. We just hand them a hot papa rellena and say, "Here, taste this!"*

Raúl: *We haven't found a "victim" yet who didn't end up loving them!*

Papa Rellena
Fried Stuffed Potatoes

. . . .

INGREDIENTS

Serves 4 to 6

4   large potatoes, peeled and quartered

½   teaspoon salt

2   tablespoons warm milk

Cuban Seasoned Ground Beef (page 42) or Picadillo (page 124)

2   eggs, beaten with 1 tablespoon water

1   cup dry bread crumbs mixed with ¼ cup flour

Peanut, vegetable, or corn oil for frying

1. Boil potatoes until they are fully cooked. Drain. Mash the potatoes by hand (do not whip with an electric mixer) with the salt and about 2 tablespoons of warm milk—do not add any butter or oil—and let cool just enough so that you can handle them. Lightly grease your hands. Grab a handful of mashed potatoes, and make a little bowl by pressing in with your fingers. Stuff the indentation in each half with Cuban Seasoned Ground Beef (page 42) or Picadillo (page 124). Now that you did such a great job with the first one, set this one aside and do another. Then bring the two halves together and smooth to make a round ball, about the size of an overstuffed golf ball.

2. Beat the eggs with water in a mixing bowl until frothy. Dip the

rellena into the beaten egg, then roll in the bread crumb/flour mixture until lightly covered. Dip a second time and roll again in bread crumbs to coat thoroughly.

IMPORTANT: Cover and refrigerate the balls for at least 4 hours before proceeding to the next step.

Instructions for pan frying:

In a large frying pan, add enough vegetable oil to cover half the ball at a time. Heat the oil to the frying stage, about 360 to 375 degrees F. Drop each papa rellena into the hot oil. Let the bottom half cook for about 2 minutes, or until golden brown. Turn the balls and cook the other half in the same way.

Instructions for deep-fat frying:

Heat the oil to 375 degrees F. Place a single layer of papas rellenas in the basket, drop into the oil, and cook for about 2 to 3 minutes, or until golden brown. Be careful not to overcook. Follow the manufacturer's instructions for your deep fat fryer.

(continued on next page)

Papa Rellena (continuation)
Fried Stuffed Potatoes

. . . .

Cuban Seasoned Ground Beef

INGREDIENTS

Serves 4 to 6

1	cup finely chopped onions
1	cup finely chopped green pepper
2	tablespoons olive oil
3	cloves garlic, minced
1	pound ground beef
½	teaspoon salt
1	teaspoon ground cumin
½	teaspoon freshly grated black pepper
1	tablespoon lime juice

1. Sauté the onions and green pepper in olive oil until the onions are limp. Add remaining ingredients and sauté until the meat is completely cooked. Drain off excess fat and let cool.

PEPPERS USED IN CUBAN COOKING

*W*HEN MANY PEOPLE *think of Latin cuisine they think peppers, and most of their thoughts lead them to some very hot peppers! However, in most Cuban cuisine, the peppers used are very tame. The typical pepper used in Cuba is the cachucha, a small and very mild green pepper. It is very similar in flavor and texture to a sweet bell pepper, which is the pepper to use if you can't get cachucha peppers in your area.*

It's interesting that one of the hottest peppers—the habanero, named after Havana—was probably developed in Cuba but is rarely used in Cuban cooking. The fiery habaneros used in Central American dishes are usually grown in the Yucatán Peninsula of Mexico and Belize. You occasionally see a small amount of habanero pepper in a picante sauce for fish or seafood, or in congri. Even then, this spicy pepper is more typical of Cuba Oriente dishes than anywhere else in Cuba.

Raúl: *Cuban tamales are a great taste treat. We love to eat them just about any time. In a Cuban tamal, the meat is mixed in with the dough and not used as a filling as in most Mexican tamales.*

Jorge: *In Cuba they use a type of field (or dent) corn; it's not as sweet and it's mealier than the sweet corn we eat in the U.S.*

Glenn: *If you have a friendly farmer nearby, you may be able to buy some.*

Raúl: *But please note— you need fresh field corn, NOT the dried stuff they feed to the cattle! You'd have to find a farmer with a field who would let you pick it fresh off the stalk.*

Glenn: *The easy way? Use sweet corn. The masa flour tends to dampen the sweetness.*

Jorge: *We've even used frozen corn when fresh corn on the cob wasn't available! The difference in taste is very slight.*

Raúl: *Most people (even die-hard Cubans) wouldn't know the difference!*

Tamales de Carne de Cerdo

Pork Tamales

. . . .

INGREDIENTS

1½	pounds pork in chunks
	Pinch of salt
	Water to cover meat
2	whole peeled garlic cloves
1	tablespoon vinegar
3	cups ground fresh or frozen corn
¾	cup lard, butter, or shortening
2½	cups chicken broth, warm
2½	cups masa harina (a finely ground corn flour used for tamales—see "Sources")
1	teaspoon Bijol powder for color (or substitute yellow food coloring)
2	cups finely chopped onion
2	cups finely chopped green pepper
	Olive oil for sautéing
5	cloves garlic, minced
½	(6-ounce) can tomato paste
½	cup warm water
½	cup red or white wine
	Juice of 1 large lemon

1   teaspoon salt

½   teaspoon freshly ground black pepper

    Corn husks (soak dried corn husks in hot water before using)

1. For meat, you need pork with plenty of fat, either well marbled or with a fat layer or both. We've had good luck with de-boned country-style pork ribs. Or have the butcher cut something to order.

2. Cut the pork up into smaller pieces—no more than 2 inches thick and 3 inches long. Add a pinch of salt and place in a 3-quart saucepan. Add water to just barely cover the meat. Add garlic cloves and vinegar. Bring to a boil, reduce heat to low, and simmer, uncovered, until all of the water has boiled away. Be sure to keep an eye on it! This process will render some of the fat out of the meat.

3. Fry the pork pieces in this rendered fat just until lightly brown but NOT too crispy! The meat should be tender and stringy. Remove the meat. Trim off any excess fat (there shouldn't be any) and break the meat into small shreds. Set aside.

4. Slice the kernels off a cob of fresh sweet corn until you have 3 cups (or use frozen corn). Quickly grind the corn in a food processor with your choice of fat (lard, butter, or shortening) until you get a very coarse mixture with visible corn kernels. Don't over-process!

5. Remove the corn from the processor and place in a large (8-quart) stockpot. Blend warm chicken broth and 2 cups masa harina into the ground corn. Add the Bijol powder to give it a nice yellow color.

6. Sauté the onion and green pepper in olive oil at medium heat, stirring occasionally, until the onion is soft. Add garlic and continue to sauté for 2 to 3 minutes. Do not drain off excess oil! Mix tomato paste in warm water and add it and the wine to the vegetables. Simmer for about 10 minutes.

7. Add the pork and vegetable mixture to the corn mixture in the stockpot. Add lemon juice, salt, and pepper, and stir. Cook the mixture on low heat, stirring frequently (don't let it burn!) until it thickens—about 20 minutes. Add more masa as necessary to make a stiff but pliable paste. Taste and add salt if needed. Remove from heat and let cool.

8. To make the tamales, take 2 corn husks and overlap them flat on the table. Put some of the meat and corn mixture in the center of the husks. Fold the husks over the filling the short way, and then fold the long way from the ends. Tie with a string.

9. Tamales are best cooked in a large pot with about 2 inches of water in the bottom. If you have the little insert that keeps the food off the bottom, great! Add the tamales, standing them on end, and cover the pot. Bring the water to a boil and cover. Reduce heat to low and simmer/steam about 1½ to 2 hours.

(continued)

Tamales de Carne de Cerdo (continuation)
Pork Tamales

. . . .

Ham Tamales

Serves 8 to 12

1. Use the same recipe above for pork, only substitute some finely chopped ham. Don't fry the ham, but do blanch it in boiling water for 1 or 2 minutes; this will draw off any excess fat and reduce some of the "hammy-ness." (If you have an excellent-tasting premium ham, you can omit this step.) Add the ham to the corn mixture as the last addition before filling the husks.

DRESSED AND READY TO GO
It's not a Cuban tamale without the fancy jacket and tie.

TAMALES

*W*ALK INTO ANY *small store or restaurant in Miami and you're going to find a real treat: tamales. Tamales are a great appetizer or side dish, and three make a very filling meal all by themselves. Cuban tamales are quite different from their Mexican cousins. Like most Cuban food, Cuban tamales are highly spiced but* NOT SPICY HOT. *Good Cuban tamales are made with freshly ground corn, and the meat (always pieces of ham, pork, or sometimes chicken) is mixed into the dough. In Miami, very good tamales can be purchased cheaply. Many families don't make their own because it's so much easier to buy them! Together we've eaten thousands of tamales from large restaurants and little* tiendas *all over Miami. We know a good tamale when we taste one!*

ENSALADA DE AGUACATE Y PIÑA
A fresh avocado and pineapple salad stops
hunger with the first bite! (Recipe page 52.)

Salads

Raúl: *You see this salad at just about every Cuban party. It's a simple, basic salad that includes white onions and ripe red tomatoes—things a typical Cuban would have in the garden.*

Jorge: *The key to this salad is getting a good crisp head of lettuce. The radishes also give this salad a nice bite.*

Glenn: *You know, sometimes the simple dishes taste the best.*

Jorge: *Or just bring back the best memories of Cuba!*

Raúl: *Let's all dream a little dream of Havana . . .*

Ensalada Cubana Típica
Typical Cuban Salad

. . . .

INGREDIENTS

Serves 6 to 8

2   ripe red tomatoes, cut in wedges

1   white onion, sliced thin

1   head iceberg lettuce, torn in pieces by hand

6   to 8 radishes, sliced thin

4   cloves garlic

1   teaspoon salt

¼   teaspoon pepper

½   cup olive oil

¼   cup white vinegar

¼   cup fresh lime juice

1. Toss together tomatoes, onion, lettuce, and radishes; place in the refrigerator to chill. Use a mortar and pestle to mash the garlic with the salt and pepper. Pour the olive oil, vinegar, and lime juice in a small bowl. Add the crushed garlic and whisk together thoroughly. You can also use a blender to emulsify the oil and liquids.

2. Just before serving, gradually add the dressing, a little at a time, while you toss the salad with a large salad fork. Add just enough dressing to cover the salad—more or less to your own taste.

Glenn: *This great Cuban salad blends the sweetness of pineapple with the sour flavor of oil and vinegar.*

Raúl: *We know it sounds strange, but it tastes great!*

Jorge: *Make sure to use a good Spanish olive oil.*

Glenn: *For salads, an extra virgin olive oil with its lighter taste is usually the best choice.*

Jorge: *Don't forget to salt and pepper the dressing to taste. It should taste slightly salty, when applied to the salad that extra saltiness is put to very good use.*

Ensalada de Aguacate y Piña

Avocado and Pineapple Salad

. . . .

INGREDIENTS

Serves 6 to 8

⅓	cup olive oil
⅓	cup vinegar
⅓	cup orange juice
⅓	cup sugar
	Salt and pepper to taste
1	head iceberg lettuce, shredded
2	cups of fresh ripe pineapple chunks
1	medium sweet red onion, sliced thin
1	large Florida avocado, peeled and sliced
1–2	Fresh limes

1. Combine olive oil, vinegar, orange juice, and sugar in a blender until smooth. Add salt and pepper to this mixture to taste. Lightly toss the lettuce, pineapple, and red onion together. Pour on the oil and vinegar mixture until everything is well coated. Adjust the amount used to your own preference, more or less.

2. Garnish individual salads with several avocado slices lightly seasoned with salt and pepper and a squeeze of lime juice.

PINEAPPLES AND NUTS
The Three Guys demonstrate their food handling techniques.

THE AMERICAN INFLUENCE ON CUBAN FOOD

THE AMERICAN influence on food has been evident throughout Cuba's history, with the peak in the 1950s. American cheese (queso Americano), American white bread (pan molde), the hamburger, peanuts roasted in the shell, Vienna sausages, and Spam are just a few of the American food items that were brought to Cuba. Jorge fondly remembers going to the two-story Woolworth's store in Havana with his sister, where he would enjoy a delicious grilled cheese sandwich made with sliced white bread and American cheese. Cubans may have received their inspiration from the United States, but they soon made several changes and improvements to give even these traditional American foods a Latin flavor!

53

Jorge: *We've been told …*

Glenn: *… by the Food Police, and you know who you are out there …*

Jorge: *… that Cuban food is unhealthy …*

Glenn: *… by the Food Police.*

Jorge: *"Where's the salads?" they cry.*

Glenn: *Again, that's the Food Police, talking.*

Jorge: *Well, just to prove them wrong, here is another delicious and healthy Cuban salad.*

Glenn: *The next time anyone from the Food Police comes over to our house, we're going to give them a big bag of dry lettuce to munch on. That will mean more of that "unhealthy" Cuban food for the rest of us!* YUM!

Ensalada de Garbanzos

Cuban Garbanzo Bean Salad

INGREDIENTS

Serves 6

1	green bell pepper, diced and blanched
1	red bell pepper, diced and blanched
1	cup diced sweet yellow onion
2	(15-ounce) cans garbanzo beans, drained
¼	cup fresh lime juice
¼	cup olive oil
1	teaspoon ground cumin
½	teaspoon salt
½	teaspoon pepper
3	garlic cloves, minced

1. Core and seed the green and red peppers. Place the peppers in a small bowl with a little water, cover with plastic wrap, and blanch in a microwave on high for approximately 90 seconds. Let the peppers cool. Dice the peppers when they are cool enough to handle.

2. Combine the peppers, onion, and garbanzo beans in a nonmetallic bowl. Use a blender to combine the lime juice, olive oil, cumin, salt, pepper, and garlic. Pour the dressing over the garbanzo bean mixture, cover and refrigerate for 1 hour or more to let the beans absorb flavor. Impress the Martha Stewart types in your neighborhood by serving the chilled salad on a fresh lettuce leaf!

Raúl: *Chicken has always been popular in Cuba.*

Jorge: *And we love our salads.*

Glenn: *So it's no surprise that Cubans have a great chicken salad recipe. The carrots and peas give this dish a lot of color for a nice presentation.*

Raúl: *And make it a lot easier to eat in the dark!*

Jorge: *With just a hint of garlic, everyone seems to love this salad.*

Glenn: *Even Raúl, flashlight and all!*

Ensalada de Pollo

Chicken Salad

· ·

INGREDIENTS

Serves 6 to 8

1½   cups diced carrots

1½   cups frozen peas

½   to ⅔ cup real mayonnaise

    Juice of one lime

1   garlic cloves, minced very fine

1   cup chopped celery

1   cup chopped onion

1   pound cooked chicken meat, diced

3   hard-boiled eggs, chopped

    Salt and pepper to taste

1. Cook the carrots and peas separately in the microwave for about 2 to 3 minutes on high. Carrots should be soft, peas dark green. Chill thoroughly in the refrigerator.

2. Mix the mayonnaise, lime juice, and garlic in a mixing bowl. Adjust the mayonnaise to get the right consistency. In a medium mixing bowl, toss the carrots, peas, celery, onion, and cooked chicken together. Add the mayonnaise mixture, a little at a time, until you get the proper consistency. Salt and pepper to taste. Gently fold in the chopped eggs. Serve well chilled on a bed of lettuce.

GAZPACHO
Glenn and Jorge's delicious Cuban
Gazpacho (recipe page 66).

Soups

Ajiaco Criollo

Country-Style Stew

. . . .

INGREDIENTS

Serves 4 to 6

3	tablespoons olive oil
4	slices smoked bacon, chopped
6	chicken thighs, bone-in, skin on
¾	pound pork loin, cut into bite-size pieces
¾	pound skirt or flank steak, cut into bite-size pieces
	Salt and pepper to taste
	Flour for dredging
3	cups beef stock
3	cups ham stock or bouillon (Goya)
1½	cups red wine
¼	cup olive oil
2	cups chopped white onion
2	cups chopped green pepper
4	garlic cloves, peeled and minced
3	tablespoons Spanish paprika
1	teaspoon salt
½	teaspoon black pepper
2	tablespoons ground cumin

Jorge: Ajiaco *is a traditional favorite of Cuban farm people.*

Glenn: *It's a rich and satisfying stew that's full of meats and vegetables—a complete meal.*

Raúl: *It is so thick you can eat it with a fork!*

Glenn: Ajiaco *brings together all of the culinary history and diversity of Cuba in one dish—the New World discoveries of corn, tomatoes, and malanga; the root vegetables from Africa; and the bacon, meats, and spices from Spain.*

Jorge: Malanga, yuca, *and* boniato, *give this dish a unique Cuban flavor. Go to your nearest Latin or Cuban grocery to find these essential ingredients!*

1   (15-ounce) can crushed tomatoes

1   bay leaf

1   cup cubed malanga

1   cup cubed boniato

1   cup cubed yuca

1   cup cubed calabaza

2   ears fresh sweet corn, husked

1   green plantain

1   semi-ripe (starting to get black) plantain

¼   cup fresh lime juice

½   cup cream

2   tablespoons cornstarch mixed with ¼ cup water

1. Heat olive oil in a skillet over medium heat. Sauté the bacon until most of the oil is released; remove bacon from pan.

2. Lightly salt and pepper the chicken, pork, and beef. Dredge in flour; brown the meat (chicken first) in the hot, bacon-flavored oil. Remove the browned meats from the oil.

3. Put all the meats (including the bacon) in a heavy 8-quart stockpot. Add the beef and ham stocks and red wine. Bring to a boil; reduce heat to low and simmer, covered, for 1 hour.

4. About 45 minutes later, heat ¼ cup olive oil in a skillet over medium heat. Sauté the onion and green pepper until the onion is translucent. Add the garlic, paprika, salt, pepper, cumin, and tomatoes, and cook for about 5 minutes. Add this vegetable mixture and the bay leaf to the meat and broth. Let simmer for 15 minutes while you peel and cut the vegetables.

5. Peel the malanga, boniato, yuca, and calabaza, and cut into cubes. Cut the corn and plantains into 2-inch chunks. Add the corn and green plantain to the simmering stew. After about 20 minutes, add the semi-ripe plantain and the lime juice; continue cooking for an additional 20 to 30 minutes. The plantain and root vegetables need to be tender!

6. Just before serving, stir in the cream. Thicken the stew slightly by whisking in the cornstarch mixed with water.

7. Serve hot in large bowls with Pan Cubano—Cuban Bread (page 184), of course!

Raúl: *This is really a Spanish recipe, but some smart Cubans stole it from the Spaniards years ago and made it a lot better.*

Jorge: *Our usual humility prevents us from naming any names. Let's just say we know three guys in Miami who really love this soup.*

Glenn: *If you use a good Spanish chorizo, you'll give your soup a hearty smoked flavor.*

Jorge: *This is a great soup, very filling! All you need is a loaf or two of fresh Cuban bread and you are in heaven!*

Caldo Gallego
White Bean Soup

. . . .

INGREDIENTS

Serves 6

2 ½	cups dry white beans
¾	cup Spanish chorizo, casings removed, and bias-sliced in 2-inch chunks
2	cups cubed smoked ham
¼	cup olive oil
2	cups chopped white onion
4	cloves garlic, minced
3	tablespoons white flour
6	cups ham broth
1	cup white wine
2	cups peeled and chopped Roma tomatoes
2	cups peeled and cubed yellow potatoes
1	teaspoon ground cumin
1	teaspoon salt
½	teaspoon black pepper
1	cup chopped fresh spinach

1. Cover dry beans with water and let stand, covered, overnight. Discard water.

2. In an 8-quart stockpot, sauté the chorizo and ham in the olive until the chorizo has colored the oil. Add the onion and sauté until limp; add minced garlic and sauté briefly. Gradually add white flour, stirring constantly to prevent those oh-so-annoying lumps!

3. Add beans, ham broth, wine, tomatoes, potatoes, cumin, salt, and pepper. Bring to a boil, then cover and simmer on low for about 2 to 3 hours. The potatoes and ham should be very tender! (The longer you simmer it, the better it tastes!)

4. Add the spinach just before the soup is done—cook only for an additional 5 minutes. Adjust seasonings to taste, and serve.

CUBAN MUSIC AND DANCE
This brightly painted mural adds a splash of color in a traditional Cuban café.

Fabada Asturiana

Hearty Spanish Bean Soup

. . . .

INGREDIENTS

Serves 6 to 8

1	yellow onion, cut in bite-size square chunks
1	green bell pepper, cut in bite-size square chunks
1	red bell pepper, cut in bite-size square chunks
¼	cup olive oil for sautéing
5	cloves of garlic, mashed with 1 teaspoon salt
6	strips bacon, chopped
4	(14½-ounce) cans of butter beans
2	cups chicken stock
¼	cup sherry
1	pound smoked ham, cut in chunks
1	teaspoon Bijol powder
	Salt and black pepper to taste
	Chunks of Spanish morcilla (blood sausage) or chorizo (optional)
2	tablespoons masa flour mixed with ½ cup water
1	cup whole milk

Jorge: *Fabada Asturiana is the signature dish of the province of Asturias in Spain.*

Glenn: *A good* fabada *is thick and flavorful, chock full of tender white beans and chunks of salty smoked ham!*

Jorge: *The bean to use in this dish is a faba bean, what is sold in the United States as a butter bean.*

Raúl: *That's where this soup gets its name—fabada!*

Glenn: *Don't confuse fabas with fava beans! The famous movie recipe that includes "fava beans and a nice Chianti" is* NOT *included in this book!*

1. Sauté the onion and peppers in olive oil in an 8-quart stockpot to release flavor, about 3 to 4 minutes. Add mashed garlic and chopped bacon during the last couple of minutes. Stir constantly to prevent the garlic from burning.

2. Add 3 cans of butter beans, including liquid. Add chicken stock, sherry, and ham chunks. Stir in the Bijol powder. Take the remaining can of butter beans, mash them, and stir into the pot. Simmer on low for about 1 hour, stirring occasionally. Add morcilla and/or chorizo chunks (optional) during the last 20 minutes of simmering.

3. Add masa flour (white flour may be substituted) mixed with water to thicken, stirring constantly. Stir in the milk, bring almost to a boil, remove from heat, and serve hot.

Jorge: *When it's hot in Miami …*

Glenn: *… this is just about every day of the year …*

Raúl: *… we like to eat something cold.*

Jorge: *Gazpacho, a cold tomato-based soup, is just the ticket. Glenn and I have developed our own recipe over the years.*

Glenn: *This recipe captures all of the fresh tastes of the garden— fresh red ripe tomatoes, crisp peppers, juicy cucumbers—combined with citrus and garlic. Just make sure the tomatoes are very ripe!*

Gazpacho de Glenn y Jorge

Glenn and Jorge's Cuban Gazpacho

. . . .

INGREDIENTS

Serves 8

2	medium onions
1	green pepper, seeded
1	red pepper, seeded
2	medium cucumbers, peeled
5	cloves garlic
5	large ripe red tomatoes
½	cup tomato juice
¼	cup olive oil
⅓	loaf of Cuban or French bread
2	tablespoons vinegar
	Juice of one lime
2	teaspoons salt, or to taste
½	teaspoon black pepper, or to taste
1	teaspoon ground cumin, or to taste
	Green pepper, seeded and diced
	Red pepper, seeded and diced

66

Cucumber, seeded (optional) and diced

Red onion, diced

Green and/or black olives

Ripe avocado, cubed

Fresh cilantro, chopped

2 jalapeño peppers

1 tablespoon lime juice

Pinch of salt

1 to 2 drops water

1. Cut all the vegetables in small chunks. If you want to be fancy or just can't stand little pieces of tomato skin, by all means peel your tomatoes! We haven't decided if we're basically lazy or just need the fiber, but we never peel our tomatoes for gazpacho. (We guess that's why we're just three regular guys from Miami!) You can also seed your cucumbers if you suffer from some sort of seed phobia.

2. Process all the vegetables in a blender in small batches with tomato juice and olive oil until you have a thick puree. (Include tomato juice and tomatoes with every batch to provide plenty of liquid.) For the last batch, soak bread in warm water and wring out excess water; add the bread and process thoroughly. Add the vinegar and lime juice. Season the puree with the salt, pepper, and cumin. Adjust to taste. Blend thoroughly in the blender. Chill in refrigerator until very cold.

3. Just before serving, garnish with chilled diced red and green peppers, cucumber, onion, olives, avocado, and some chopped cilantro.

4. For an added kick, puree the jalapeños, lime juice, salt, and water; add sparingly to each bowl just before serving, or serve at the table.

AGUACATE

The Avocado

ALTHOUGH IT SEEMS like a vegetable, the avocado (or aguacate in Spanish) is really a fruit. There are more than twenty different varieties of avocado. The large, light-skinned varieties, sometimes called "Florida" or "Anaheim," are the most popular with Cuban Americans. The Hass variety, a small, dark, thick-skinned avocado that is popular with California growers, is seldom used in Cuban households.

A ripe avocado is frequently used as a simple salad. Just slice the avocado into wedges, drizzle on a little olive oil, sprinkle with fresh lime juice, add salt and black pepper to taste. It makes a delicious and refreshing treat.

When avocados get overly ripe, many Cuban girls like to make a paste with the avocado and rub it into their hair! They leave it in for as long as they can stand it and then rinse. It's supposed to add shine and luster! Lather, rinse, repeat. Yes, but when can I stop?

Guisado de Chorizo y Papas
Chorizo and Potato Stew

. . . .

INGREDIENTS

Serves 6

2½	cups chopped onion
3	cups chopped green pepper
	Olive oil for sautéing
4	cups red potatoes, peeled, quartered and cut in bite-size pieces
4 or 5	Spanish chorizo links (about 1 pound), sliced diagonally in 1-inch pieces
5	cloves garlic mashed with ½ teaspoon salt
1½	quarts chicken broth
2	tablespoons Spanish paprika
1	teaspoon black pepper
¼	cup chopped fresh cilantro (leaves only)
2	tablespoons masa flour or cornstarch mixed with ¼ cup water

Glenn: *The key to this dish is to use a hard, dry Spanish chorizo.*

Jorge: *Do not use the Mexican chorizo, which is soft and spicy and doesn't taste anything like Spanish chorizo!*

Raúl: *This is NOT a Mexican dish!*

Glenn: *We usually use red potatoes, although we've had some good luck with the Yukon Gold variety of potatoes. They are not as starchy as regular potatoes and have a wonderful sweet flavor.*

Jorge: *Be sure to add the cilantro during the final minutes of cooking. Otherwise, you'll destroy the flavor.*

68

1. Briefly sauté the onion and green pepper in olive oil in an 8-quart stockpot. Add the potatoes and chorizo, and sauté until the potatoes are browned slightly. Stir in the mashed garlic and salt mixture; sauté for an additional 2 minutes. Add the chicken broth, paprika, and black pepper. Bring to a boil, reduce heat to low, cover, and simmer until the potatoes are soft—about 20 to 30 minutes. Add more chicken stock if necessary or if the stew becomes too thick. Add the cilantro and cook for an additional 5 minutes. Season with additional salt and pepper if necessary.

2. If the stew is too thin, make a paste out of masa flour or cornstarch and water; stir rapidly into the simmering stew, a little at a time, until you get the desired thickness.

REAL SPANISH CHORIZO
This dry-cured smoked sausage is a key ingredient in Cuban cuisine.

Potaje de Frijoles Colorados

Red Bean Potage

. . . .

INGREDIENTS

Serves 6 to 8

2½ cups dried frijoles colorados cortos, a small Spanish-style red bean

6 strips bacon, chopped

¼ cup olive oil for sautéing

2½ cups chopped onion

2½ cups chopped green pepper

6 cloves garlic, mashed

1 pound ham, cubed

1 (15-ounce) can crushed tomatoes

1 teaspoon oregano

1 tablespoon ground cumin

2 tablespoons vinegar

Juice of 1 lime

1 teaspoon salt

½ teaspoon black pepper

1 cup red wine

7 cups chicken or ham stock

Jorge: *Red beans have always been more popular in Cuba Oriente than anywhere else in Cuba.*

Glenn: *It must be the Haitian influence!*

Jorge: *There are several Cuban recipes that use red beans: Potaje de Frijoles Colorados and Congri are just two of the most popular examples.*

Glenn: *If you like ham, you will love this thick, rich soup!*

Raúl: *Hey, you can't be Cuban and not like ham!*

3 potatoes, peeled and diced

2 cups diced calabaza or butternut squash

2 tablespoons masa flour or cornstarch mixed with
   ½ cup water

Frijoles colorados cortos is a small Spanish-style red bean, sometimes called simply "small red beans" or "Mexican red beans." If you can't find any of these, you may substitute red kidney beans.

There are two ways to prepare the dryed red beans for this recipe:

A. Cover dry beans with water, bring to a boil, and cook for 2 minutes. Remove from heat, cover, and let stand overnight. Discard water.

B. Cover the beans with water in a 3-quart saucepan. Bring to a boil, reduce heat to medium low, cover, and cook until tender, about 1 hour. Drain.

1. When beans are ready to use in the recipe, sauté the bacon in olive oil in an 8-quart stockpot until it begins to brown. Add the onion and green pepper and sauté until the onions are tender. Add the garlic and ham and cook another 1 to 2 minutes. Add the red beans, crushed tomatoes, oregano, cumin, vinegar, lime juice, salt, pepper, red wine, and chicken or ham stock. Bring to a boil; add the diced potatoes and calabaza. Stir gently and let the soup come to a boil again. Reduce heat to low, cover, and simmer until the potatoes and calabaza are fully cooked and fork-tender—about 40 minutes.

2. Remove 2 cups of the mixture (make sure to get plenty of solids) and puree in a blender or food processor. Stir masa flour (or cornstarch) mixed with water into the soup to thicken it. Add the puree and stir gently. Add more salt and pepper to taste. Serve hot.

Glenn: *Although we can't really make any medical claims, this is the soup to eat if you have a bad head cold.*

Jorge: *It's a much better remedy than chicken soup!*

Glenn: *The only tricky part to this soup is whisking in the eggs at the end. You need to whisk the soup very rapidly to prevent the eggs from cooking into one thick mess!*

Jorge: *Use Cuban bread if you have it. Otherwise you may substitute French bread. Just don't use common white bread—it should never be used in cooking!*

Glenn: *Oh, one more thing. When we say separate the eggs, we don't mean that you should put each of them in a different room. That should only be necessary if your eggs are constantly fighting and just won't listen to reason.*

Sopa de Ajo
Garlic Soup

. . . .

INGREDIENTS

Serves 4 to 6

6	slices Cuban bread, cubed
3	tablespoons olive oil
12	garlic cloves, peeled and minced
1	(28-ounce) can peeled whole tomatoes, drained and chopped
1	teaspoon paprika
1	bay leaf
4	cups chicken broth
¼	cup sherry
	Salt and black pepper to taste
6	eggs
	Parsley for garnish

1. Sauté cubes of bread in hot oil in an 8-quart stockpot until they just begin to brown. Stir in the minced garlic and sauté for another 1 to 2 minutes, just long enough to cook the garlic slightly. Use a wooden spoon to mash the garlic and bread together. Add tomatoes, paprika, bay leaf, chicken broth, and sherry. Bring to a boil, reduce heat to low and simmer for 1 hour. Salt and pepper to taste.

2. Separate the eggs; add 3 tablespoons of the hot broth to the egg yolks, beating constantly, to temper them. Add egg yolks to the broth and whisk in rapidly until smooth. Quickly whisk in the unbeaten egg whites until mixed completely. Bring the soup back to a boil and immediately remove from heat. Garnish with parsley and serve.

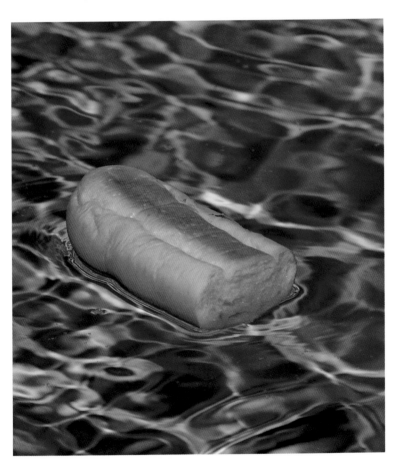

Raúl: *This is the Cuban version of a soup that is popular all over the United States.*

Glenn: *We're not sure exactly who had this soup first, but the Cuban version is very distinctive.*

Jorge: *The secret ingredient? Calabaza.*

Glenn: *Jorge's mom uses chunks of real calabaza. If you have a Mexican or Latin market in your town, chances are they have calabaza. If you can't find calabaza in your area, you can use butternut squash instead.*

Sopa de Chicharos
Cuban Split Pea Soup

. . . .

INGREDIENTS

Serves 6

1	pound dried split peas
2	cups chopped white onion
2	cups chopped green pepper
¼	cup olive oil for sautéing
5	cloves garlic, minced
3	tablespoons white flour
1	leftover ham bone with plenty of meat attached
4½	cups water
4½	cups chicken broth
1	cup white wine
1½	cups peeled and cubed calabaza or butternut squash
1	teaspoon Accent
2	teaspoons ground cumin
¼	cup butter

Salt and black pepper to taste

2   tablespoons masa flour or cornstarch mixed with ½ cup
    water (optional)

1. Wash split peas in water, being careful to remove any grit or bad peas.

2. Sauté the onion and green pepper with a little olive oil in a sauté pan. Add garlic and flour and sauté for another 1 to 2 minutes, stirring constantly.

3. Place the ham bone in an 8-quart stockpot. Add peas, onion/pepper/garlic mixture, water, chicken broth and wine. Bring to a boil, reduce heat to low, and simmer until the peas are very tender and the ham is starting to fall off the bone—approximately 2 hours. Remove the ham bone, trim all usable meat from the bone, cut into small bite-size chunks, and set aside. Discard bone, excess fat, and gristle.

4. Add the calabaza to the pot and continue cooking until the calabaza is soft, approximately 20 to 30 minutes. Place the cooked soup in a blender or food processor and puree in small batches. Be careful, the soup is hot! Return puree to the pot and add the ham chunks, Accent, cumin, and butter. Simmer an additional 20 to 30 minutes. Season to taste with salt and pepper.

5. If the mixture is too thin for your taste, thicken with a little cornstarch dissolved in water.

Glenn: *Plantain soup is a richly flavored chicken-based soup. If your family is sick of American chicken noodle soup …*

Jorge: *… and whose family isn't?…*

Glenn: *… why not try the Cuban version, a hearty soup that includes tender chunks of plantain.*

Raúl: *At our house we eat it a lot! The whole house smells great whenever we cook it!*

Jorge: *And so do the chefs!*

Glenn: *At least the dogs seem to think so …*

Sopa de Plátanos

Plantain Soup

· · · · · · · · · · · · · · · · ·

INGREDIENTS

Serves 6

- 1 cup diced celery
- 1 cup finely chopped onion
- 1½ cups shredded carrots
- ¼ cup olive oil for sautéing
- 5 cloves garlic, minced
- 6 cups chicken stock
- 2 large green plantains, peeled, and sliced in 1-inch pieces
- 1 tablespoon ground cumin
- 1 teaspoon Bijol powder
- 1 bay leaf
  Salt and black pepper to taste
- ½ cup chopped cilantro

1. Sauté celery, onion, and carrots in olive oil in an 8-quart stockpot until onions are soft and translucent. Stir in the minced garlic and sauté an additional minute. Pour in chicken stock and bring to a boil. Add plantains, cumin, Bijol powder, and bay leaf. Bring back to a boil, reduce heat to low, cover, and simmer for about 1 hour, or until the plantains are tender. Remove and discard bay leaf.

2. With a slotted spoon, remove 1 cup of the vegetables from the soup and puree in a food processor or blender. Add puree back into the soup and continue cooking on low heat for 5 additional minutes. Season with salt and pepper. Taste it. Adjust seasonings as necessary. Stir in chopped cilantro. Serve in stoneware bowls garnished with sprigs of cilantro.

Raúl: *Every Cuban had a mother or grandmother who prepared her own special chicken soup.*

Jorge: *My mother is still making hers—and it's delicious!*

Raúl: *This recipe includes yuca and plantains. Take care not to overcook the vegetables or they will completely disintegrate.*

Jorge: *It gets cold enough in Miami some winters that we end up eating a lot of this soup just to warm up.*

Glenn: *Cold in Miami? While I'm freezing in Minnesota at 20 degrees below zero, I really feel sorry for my two brothers-in-law when they can't use Jorge's swimming pool!*

Sopa de Pollo

Chicken Soup

INGREDIENTS

Serves 4 to 6

1	bunch green onions, chopped
1	small bunch cilantro, chopped
1	tablespoon ground cumin
3	tablespoons olive oil for sautéing
3	tablespoons white flour
6	cups chicken stock
8	chicken thighs
1	yuca, peeled and cut into 1-inch cubes
1	cup cubed calabaza
2	red potatoes, unpeeled, cut into chunks
2	plantains, peeled, halved, and sliced into thirds
½	cup fresh lemon juice
	Salt and black pepper to taste
	Red onion, sliced

1. Briefly sauté green onions, cilantro (save some for garnish), and cumin in olive oil. Quickly whisk in the flour, stirring thoroughly to avoid lumps. Immediately add 1 cup chicken stock, and continue to whisk until well blended. Remove from heat. Set this chicken stock/onion/cilantro mixture aside.

2. Place chicken and remaining chicken stock in an 8-quart stockpot. Bring to a boil, reduce heat to low, cover, and simmer for 20 minutes. Add the yuca, calabaza, potatoes, and plantains; continue to simmer for about 40 minutes, or until the vegetables are tender.

3. Remove the chicken thighs from the soup and run under cold water to cool. Skin and de-bone the chicken, breaking it into bite-size pieces. Return the chicken pieces to the simmering broth.

4. Add the chicken stock/onion/cilantro mixture and the lemon juice to the soup and stir thoroughly. Continue cooking until the soup is hot and ready to serve. Salt and pepper to taste. Garnish with chopped cilantro and sliced mild red onion.

AREPAS
A cheesy Cuban sandwich
made with cornmeal pancakes.
(Recipe page 82)

Sandwiches

Glenn: Arepas *are delicious little cornmeal pancakes, a very popular treat on street corners in Colombia.*

Raúl: *You also see them all over Miami! They are very popular at festivals and other events.*

Glenn: *The traditional* arepa *served at lunch counters in Miami has two cornmeal pancakes with a layer of cheese inside. The pancakes are slightly sweet and have a delicious corn flavor. They're usually smeared with butter and cooked on a griddle until they're lightly browned and crisp.*

Jorge: *Most restaurants use a mild mozzarella or Swiss cheese. We've had good luck with a baby Swiss—the one without the holes.*

Glenn: *You can also use Monterey Jack with good results.*

Arepas

Cornmeal Pancakes

. . . .

INGREDIENTS

Serves 6 to 8

1	cup milk
5	tablespoons butter
1	cup frozen corn kernels
1	cup arepa flour, or 1 cup finely ground yellow cornmeal
¼	teaspoon salt
⅓	cup sugar
1	cup grated mozzarella cheese
½	cup water (approximately)
	Mild Swiss cheese, sliced

1. Bring the milk to a boil in a small pan. Add butter. Let stand and cool slightly.

2. Grind frozen yellow corn kernels in a food processor. You can find arepa flour at many Latin and Mexican markets. If there isn't one near you, use finely ground yellow cornmeal. In a large bowl, mix the ground corn, arepa flour or cornmeal, salt, sugar, and mozzarella. Make a well in the center and gradually add the hot milk and butter mixture. Stir until there are no lumps. Work the dough until it is smooth and sticky. Add water as necessary if the dough is too thick.

3. Place dough on a lightly floured surface and use a rolling pin to roll it out to about ½ inch thickness. Cut out the arepas with a large cookie cutter—about 3 inches in diameter. (We've had good luck using a small straight-edged bowl.)

4. Heat a lightly buttered griddle to medium. Cook the arepas in batches until crispy and golden brown on each side. Immediately place a slice or two of cheese on one arepa and cover with another to make a sandwich. Reduce heat to low and continue cooking until the cheese melts, flipping a few times.

5. You may also make the pancakes only and store them in the refrigerator or freezer until ready to serve. Just lightly butter two pancakes, put a slice of cheese in between, and heat on the griddle at low heat until the cheese melts.

TIP: We also have made these by thinning out the batter slightly with a little water so that it can be spooned directly onto a griddle, like a pancake. This saves all the work of rolling out and cutting!

83

Glenn: *This sandwich was named for Elena Ruz, a young lady who frequented the El Carmelo restaurant in the Vedado neighborhood of Havana in the 1930s.*

Jorge: *Elena had a thing for pavo, or turkey, and she was very particular about the way the chef prepared her sandwich.*

Raúl: *This young lady knew what she wanted and she wasn't afraid to ask for it!*

Jorge: *The bread had to be American-style white, with the crust removed. It had to be lightly toasted and NOT flattened in the plancha like a Cuban sandwich. The cream cheese had to be softened and spread evenly without tearing the bread.*

Glenn: *After many visits, Elena asked the waiter to put her sandwich on the menu. The next her namesake sandwich appeared on the menu.*

Jorge: *Someday we'd like to have a sandwich named after us...*

Raúl: *... probably something with plenty of spice and a lot of tongue!*

Elena Ruz

Cuban Turkey Sandwich

. . . .

INGREDIENTS

Makes 4 sandwiches

8	slices white bread, crusts removed
4 to 5	ounces cream cheese, room temperature
4	tablespoons strawberry jam or guava jelly
8	ounces sliced roast turkey breast
	Pinch of salt to taste

1. Cut the crust from the bread and lightly toast in an electric toaster. The bread should be slightly dry and crisp, but NOT brown.

2. Spread a thin layer of softened cream cheese on one piece of bread and strawberry jam on the other. Arrange the turkey slices on the cream-cheese-covered slice and add a pinch of salt. (No salt is necessary if you are using some type of prepared turkey sandwich meat, but you know you shouldn't be doing that!)

3. Bring the two halves together using the traditional sandwich method! You know, the one where one piece of bread goes pretty much directly on top of the other? Slice diagonally and serve with some mariquitas or French fries.

Some places in Miami make these with guava jelly, a very tasty variation!

Pan con Lechón

Roast Pork Sandwich

. . . .

INGREDIENTS

Serves 4

4   individual Cuban bread loaves or French bread

4   tablespoons butter, softened

1   pound pork roast (page 120), shredded

1   onion, sliced thin

   Mojo (page 178)

1. Slice the bread loaves in half. Butter both sides of each loaf of bread.

2. The pork needs to be warm. Heat some up in a frying pan with a dash of oil. Shred the pork with a meat cleaver. Layer the shredded pork onto the bread and cover with a single layer of sliced raw onion. Sprinkle with a little Mojo. Slice the sandwich in half diagonally and serve.

Raúl: *One more great use for leftover Lechón Asado (pork roast) is another great Cuban sandwich: Pan con Lechón.*

Glenn: *It's a simple sandwich—just pork, onions, and plenty of tangy Mojo sauce.*

Jorge: *Pan con Lechón sandwiches are very popular all over Miami. If you see someone selling them on a street corner, don't pass them up; they are a real treat and usually only cost a buck or two.*

Glenn: *If you just can't make it to Miami, why not make some at home?*

Jorge: *Like many things that came to Cuba by way of other cultures, the hamburger soon became a popular favorite. Although there was never a McDonald's in Havana, we do have the United States to thank for introducing this popular favorite.*

Glenn: *Finding the meat a little bland, some enterprising Cubans decided to "kick it up a notch."*

Jorge: *You mean Emeril is Cuban? I thought he was Portuguese!*

Raúl: *The best way to make this is with a food processor and a chopping blade.*

Glenn: *Use the blade to finely grind the meats, garlic, and onion into a smooth mixture.*

Frita Cubana

Cuban Hamburger

. . . .

INGREDIENTS

Makes 6 to 8 generous patties

In Miami, the Frita Cubana is very popular, and there are several restaurants that specialize in it.

Burgers

1	pound ground beef
¾	pound ground pork
4	cloves mashed and finely minced garlic
⅓	cup grated onion
2	tablespoons ketchup
¾	teaspoon ground cumin
1½	teaspoons sweet Spanish paprika
	Salt & pepper cooked patties to taste
6 to 8	American-style hamburger or steak buns

Topping

6 to 8	cups freshly fried shoestring potatoes
	Shredded lettuce
	Sliced raw onion
	Glenn's Not-So-Secret Sauce (see recipe below)

1. Use a food processor with a chopping blade to grind together the meats, minced garlic, and onion. Blend in the ketchup, cumin, and paprika. Remove the meat mixture from the food processor and form by hand into thin round patties. Cook on a flat griddle or in a frying pan. Fritas should be cooked to medium-well done, but don't overcook—they should still be nice and juicy.

2. While the fritas are frying, use a deep fat fryer or frying pan with a couple inches of vegetable oil to fry the shoestring potatoes. Drain on paper towels and lightly salt. Keep warm.

3. Serve each frita on a traditional American hamburger bun. Splash plenty of Glenn's Not-So-Secret Sauce on the bun and the patty.

4. Place the patty on the bun, cover with sliced lettuce and onion, and pile high with fresh, hot shoe-string style fried potatoes—yes, inside the bun, ON TOP of the meat! Splash a little extra sauce on the fries—you'll be glad you did!

5. Serve with additional fries on the plate.

Glenn's Not-So-Secret Sauce

INGREDIENTS

1	(6-ounce) can tomato paste
1½	cups water
1	teaspoon ground cumin
1½	teaspoons sweet Spanish paprika
1	teaspoon garlic powder
¼	cup sugar
¼	cup white vinegar
1	teaspoon salt

1. Mix all of the ingredients together in a two-quart saucepan. Bring to a boil, stirring constantly. Reduce heat to low and simmer, stirring occasionally, for 10 to 15 minutes. Remove from heat and let cool. Use in the Frita Cubana recipe above.

Glenn: *I've been working on duplicating the "Secret Sauce" at my favorite Miami frita restaurant. I don't know that I'll ever get it exactly right, but this one comes really close!*

Raúl: *But Glenn, if we put this recipe in the cookbook, it won't be a secret anymore!*

Glenn: *I've been working on a solution to that, Raúl. It involves a blindfold and some creative kitchen work…*

Jorge: *Hey, if you won't tell anyone, neither will we!*

Jorge: *To make the traditional toasted and flattened Cuban sandwich, restaurants use a special press called a* plancha.

Glenn: *We've had good success pressing them on a griddle with a bacon press or heavy cast-iron pan. We've even seen people use a brick wrapped in aluminum foil!*

Raúl: *Of course, there is only one bread that works best and that's Cuban bread. If you can't get your hands on any, a fresh loaf of French bread can be substituted.*

Glenn: *Ideally, you need a loaf that is crusty on the outside and soft in the middle.*

Jorge: *Never use a baguette, which is too narrow and too hard to press correctly!*

Sándwich Cubano
Cuban Sandwich

. . . .

INGREDIENTS

Makes 4 large sandwiches

	Cuban bread (or substitute French bread if you must, but NOT a baguette!)
	Butter, softened
	Dill pickles, sliced
1	pound Lechón Asado, sliced
1	pound good-quality ham, sliced
½	pound Swiss cheese, sliced (use a mild Swiss; we like baby Swiss—it has only a few holes)
	Yellow mustard (optional)
	Mayonnaise (optional)

1. Preheat a griddle or large sauté pan. Cut the bread into sections about 8 inches long. Cut these in half and spread butter on both halves (inside). Make each sandwich with the ingredients in this order: pickles, roasted pork, ham, and cheese. Be generous!

2. Place the sandwich on a lightly greased hot griddle or sauté pan. Place a heavy iron skillet or bacon press on top of the sandwich to flatten. Put a little muscle into it! You really want to smash the sandwich, compressing the bread to about a third of its original size!

3. Grill the sandwiches for 2 to 3 minutes on each side, until the cheese is melted and the bread is golden. Make sure your griddle or sauté pan is not TOO HOT! Otherwise, the crust will burn before the cheese melts. Slice the sandwich in half diagonally and serve.

TIP: Let your meats and cheese come to room temperature. This way you avoid burning the bread, and the cheese melts perfectly! This is especially helpful when you have a lot of meat in your sandwich. For extra flavor, sprinkle a little Mojo sauce (page 178) on the meat before adding the cheese. Using mustard or mayonnaise is a personal choice. We find that the best Cuban sandwiches don't need either ingredient. The butter, natural meat juices—and, yes, even the pickle juice—provide all of the moistness and flavor needed.

Medianoche
Midnight Sandwich

. . . .

1. Use all the same ingredients as the Cuban sandwich, except use a medianoche bread loaf. This sweeter, smaller-sized bread is the only difference between a Medianoche and a Cuban Sandwich!

HISTORY OF THE CUBAN SANDWICH

*N*o one is certain exactly where and when the Cuban sandwich was invented. We do know that a type of Cuban sandwich called a sandwich mixto was common on cafeteria and restaurant menus in Cuba by the 1930s, and there is some evidence of them as early as the turn of the century. The mixto was very popular with workers in Cuba's sugar mills. People set up restaurants inside the mills and sold the sandwiches to the workers on their lunch breaks. Who first brought the Cuban sandwich to the United States? Wow, do you like a good argument? This is one topic on which there will never be an agreement.

MORE THAN ONE WAY TO MAKE A CUBAN SANDWICH

*I*n the province of Oriente, the eastern part of Cuba, they eat a different version of the Cuban sandwich. It is exactly like the traditional Cuban sandwich, but the bread is rubbed with roasted garlic first.

Tampa Cubans claim to have invented the Cuban sandwich (we're not even going to go there!), and in Tampa it isn't a Cuban sandwich without Genoa salami! However, that is an addition that is unique to Tampa. You won't find salami on a Cuban sandwich in just about any other city. Most likely this came about because in the early days of Ybor City, where the Cuban sandwich was popularized, the only ethnic group as numerous as the Cubans was the Italians. So it's understandable that there was a little blending of the two cultures, at least when it came to Genoa salami on a Cuban sandwich. In Key West, a Cuban sandwich always includes lettuce and tomato. They also like to call it something besides a Cuban sandwich, usually a Key West Cuban Mix or something similar. Could a Cuban sandwich by any other name taste as sweet?

91

HUEVOS HABANEROS
Enjoy some spicy Havana Eggs
for breakfast or anytime!
(Recipe page 96.)

Eggs

Raúl: *Okay, an egg is running down a street in Havana and a crowd of hungry Cubans is chasing him. Up ahead he sees a pork chop leisurely walking along the avenue. As he passes the pork chop, he yells, "Run for your life! There's a bunch of hungry Cubans coming!"*

Glenn: *The pork chop barely looks up and, if anything, he slows his pace a bit. "Are you crazy," yells the egg. "They're right behind you. This is your last chance! Run!"*

Jorge: *And the pork chop says, "I don't have to run. It's been so long since any of those Cubans have seen me, they won't even recognize me!"*

Glenn: *The people in Cuba today cannot enjoy the foods that Americans take for granted. We hope that some day the burden of communism is lifted and the Cuban people can enjoy these delicious recipes once again!*

Huevos a la Flamenco

Flamenco-Style Eggs

. . . .

INGREDIENTS

Serves 4

1	cup chopped onion
½	cup diced carrots
	Olive oil for sautéing
3	cloves of garlic, mashed
¼	cup tomato sauce
½	cup green peas
½	cup canned garbanzo beans
	Salt and pepper to taste

4	slices of ham, cut to fit custard cups
4	chorizo sausage links, sliced
8	eggs
	Spanish sweet paprika for garnish

1. Preheat oven to 375 degrees F.

2. Sauté the onion and carrots in olive oil on medium heat until the onions are limp. Add the mashed garlic. Continue to sauté for a few minutes, stirring occasionally. Add the tomato sauce, peas, and garbanzo beans, and simmer on low for 15 minutes. Salt and pepper to taste.

3. Lightly butter the bottom and sides of four custard cups. Spoon some of the vegetable mixture into each—divided equally. Top with one slice of ham and several slices of chorizo. Gently break two eggs into each dish so that the eggs float on top. (Be careful not to break the yolks!) Place the dishes in the oven (we usually place the custard cups on a baking sheet or jelly roll pan) and bake for 15 to 20 minutes, or until the whites are WHITE! Traditionally the yolks are served slightly runny. However, you may cook this dish a little longer if you like hard-cooked yolks. Dust each cup with a little sweet paprika and serve immediately.

TIP: Please note that many health experts now advise against serving undercooked eggs. If you like them runny, we recommend that you use pasteurized eggs to help reduce the risk.

Jorge: *Huevos Habaneros makes a great brunch or formal breakfast dish. Many people have never tried baking eggs in the oven, but this is one dish that is very easy to do.*

Raúl: *You can put it in the oven and work on something else—like drinking a beer—while it's cooking.*

Glenn: *We like to eat it on Sunday mornings during football season.*

Raúl: *Go Dolphins!*

Glenn: *A hearty breakfast of Huevos Habaneros, fried chorizo, and Cuban bread is the perfect way to stoke up before the big game!*

Jorge: *And you don't even have to like football to love this dish!*

Huevos Habaneros
Havana Eggs
· ·

INGREDIENTS

Serves 4

1   cup chopped onion

1   cup red bell pepper, cored and chopped

1   cup green bell pepper, cored and chopped

    Olive oil for sautéing

3   cloves garlic mashed with ½ teaspoon salt and ¼ teaspoon black peppercorns

3   tablespoons white wine

1   cup peeled, cored, and chopped fresh tomato

1   teaspoon ground cumin

    Salt and pepper to taste

8   eggs

4   tablespoons butter

    Spanish sweet paprika for garnish

1. Preheat oven to 375 degrees F.

2. Make a sofrito by sautéing onion and the red and green bell peppers in olive oil over low heat until the onion is translucent. Add the garlic and cook just 1 to 2 minutes more, stirring occasionally. Add the wine, tomatoes, and cumin. Cook over low heat for about 5 minutes, stirring frequently. Salt and pepper to taste.

3. Lightly butter the bottom and sides of four custard cups. Set aside about 3/4 cup of sofrito to use as a garnish. Spoon remaining sofrito into four cups, divided equally. Gently break 2 eggs into each dish on top of the sofrito. (Be careful not to break the yolks!) Place 1 tablespoon of butter on top of the eggs in each dish. Place the dishes in the oven (we usually place the custard cups on a baking sheet or jelly roll pan) and bake for 15 to 20 minutes, or until the whites are WHITE! Traditionally the yolks are served soft and runny. However, you may cook this dish a little longer if you like hard-cooked yolks. Garnish the top of the eggs with some of the reserved sofrito, sprinkle a little paprika on top of each dish and serve immediately.

TIP: Please note that many health experts now advise against serving undercooked eggs. If you like them runny, we recommend that you use pasteurized eggs to help reduce the risk.

Jorge: *We frequently get party invitations like this: "You guys are invited and, oh yeah, could you please bring one of your (wonderful, delightful, curious) Cuban dishes for potluck?"*

Raúl: *Sometimes I think people like to see our food more than they like to see us!*

Glenn: *One day we received one of those invitations. "We'd love to have chorizo pie!" Several times over the years, we remembered eating a chorizo pie that was a lot like a quiche.*

Raúl: *Do real Cuban guys eat quiche? I don't think so!*

Glenn: *In any case, we went into the kitchen to try to re-create this "quiche-like" pie.*

Jorge: *And that's how this recipe was born! It has become a party favorite, especially for brunches.*

Raúl: *Just don't tell the Cuban guys at your party that they're eating quiche!*

Pastel de Chorizo
Cuban Chorizo Pie
. . . .

INGREDIENTS

Serves 12 to 14 (makes 2 9-inch pies)

1	pound Portuguese-style chorizo sausage (or substitute a mild Mexican chorizo)
1½	cups chopped yellow onion
4	cloves of garlic, minced
2	cups green pepper, chopped
4	tablespoons butter
14	extra large eggs
2	unbaked Pillsbury pie crusts
1	pint heavy cream
¾	teaspoon salt
½	teaspoon pepper
1	teaspoon ground cumin
1½	teaspoons ancho chili powder (or any very mild chili powder)
2	cups grated Monterey Jack cheese
	Parsley for garnish

1. Preheat oven to 450 degrees F.

2. Use a sharp knife to remove the casings from the chorizo. Lightly sauté chorizo. Drain and blot with paper towels. Sauté onions, garlic, and green pepper in butter until translucent. Drain.

3. If you love to make your own pie crust, by all means have at it! If you want to use a great and easy substitute, pick up a box of Pillsbury pie dough in the refrigerated dough section of your supermarket. Whichever way you go, use the crust to line a 9-inch pie plate. Trim the crust to fit the plate and use a fork or your fingers to make a decorative edge.

4. Beat eggs in a mixing bowl until frothy. Gradually add cream, salt, pepper, cumin, and chili powder. Crumble the chorizo and mix with sautéed garlic, onion, and green pepper. Spread an even layer on the bottom of each pie shell. Top with grated cheese. Pour the egg mixture over the top. Bake for the first 10 minutes at 450 degrees F. Reduce oven temperature to 300 degrees F and continue baking until the custard sets—about 45 to 50 minutes, or until a knife inserted into the middle comes out relatively clean. Cut into serving-size wedges and plate with a sprig of parsley. If anyone even mentions the "Q" word, play dumb!

CHURRASCO ESTILO CUBANO
Nothing's better than a juicy
Cuban-Style Skirt Steak (recipe
page 116).

Meat

Glenn: *Stuffed peppers are a traditional entrée in many cuisines. My mother used to make Mexican-style stuffed peppers with rice when I was growing up in Minneapolis.*

Raúl: *In Cuba, we mostly ate mild green peppers. Hot peppers were only used in a few dishes.*

Jorge: *This recipe has a more intense meat flavor than the recipe most Americans are used to. The wine gives the dish a very nice flavor.*

Glenn: *Sorry, Mom, but I like this one a lot better!*

Ajíes Rellenos
Stuffed Green Peppers

• •

INGREDIENTS

Serves 8

8	large whole green peppers

Sauce

2	(16-ounce) cans tomato sauce
1/3	cup red or white wine
1	tablespoon white vinegar
1/4	cup light brown sugar
1	teaspoon ground cumin
1	teaspoon salt
1/2	teaspoon pepper

Filling

2	cups white onion, chopped
1	pound ground beef
1	pound ground pork
2	tablespoons olive oil for sautéing
1	(28-ounce) can whole tomatoes, drained and chopped
3	cups day old bread (preferably Cuban) cubed

2   teaspoons salt

½   teaspoon black pepper

2   teaspoons ground cumin

1   teaspoon oregano

2   teaspoons paprika

½   cup sauce (see above)

1. Preheat the oven to 300 degrees F.

2. Wash green peppers, slice off stem end, and remove seeds and ribs. Drop the peppers into boiling water that has been lightly salted. Boil long enough to blanch—about 2 minutes—and remove. Let cool.

3. To make sauce, put all of the sauce ingredients in a three quart saucepan and whisk together until well blended. Bring to a boil, stirring constantly. Reduce heat to low and let simmer for 15-20 minutes.

4. Meanwhile, sauté onion with ground beef, ground pork, and a little olive oil until browned. DO NOT DRAIN. Stir in tomatoes and heat through. Remove from heat and stir in bread cubes, salt, pepper, cumin, oregano, paprika, and half of the sauce. Stuff peppers and place in lightly greased baking dish.

5. Pour remaining sauce over the peppers. Cover the pan with aluminum foil and bake for 30 minutes.

Jorge: *When you think of meatballs, you probably are thinking about something Italian.*

Glenn: *Don't forget Swedish meatballs.*

Raúl: *Or those little meatballs in the barbeque sauce some people serve at parties.*

Glenn: *Those are usually made out of rubber, aren't they?*

Jorge: *However, Cubans have their own version of the meatball. This is a great recipe for this Cuban treat.*

Raúl: *The key here is that Cuban meatballs are big—about the size of a small Volkswagen!*

Glenn: *That's one BIG SPICY meatball!*

Jorge: *Wrong commercial, Glenn!*

Albóndigas
Cuban Meatballs

. . . .

INGREDIENTS

Serves 4 to 6

Meatballs

2	eggs
1	cup cracker crumbs (try Cuban or Club crackers)
¼	cup milk
1½	pounds ground beef
1	teaspoon dry yellow mustard
2	teaspoons ground cumin
1	teaspoon salt
½	teaspoon pepper
½	cup finely chopped onion
½	cup finely chopped green onions
	Flour for rolling
	Olive oil for frying

Sauce

1	cup chopped onion
1	cup chopped green pepper

Olive oil for sautéing

4   cloves garlic, mashed

⅓   cup ketchup

1   tablespoon white vinegar

1   tablespoon brown sugar

½   teaspoon salt

1   (15-ounce) can tomato sauce

1. To make the meatballs, mix together the eggs, cracker crumbs, milk, ground beef, mustard, cumin, salt, pepper, and onions in a large bowl until completely blended. Use your hands—no one's watching and believe us, it's the only way! Form mixture into large balls. Roll in flour to lightly coat and sauté in olive oil until cooked through.

2. To make the sauce, sauté onion and green pepper in olive oil in a 3-quart saucepan until translucent. Add mashed garlic during the last 1 or 2 minutes of sautéing. Mop up any excess oil with a paper towel (be careful not to let the hot oil touch your fingers). Add the ketchup, vinegar, brown sugar, salt, and tomato sauce, and mix well. Add the cooked meatballs and bring to a boil. Reduce heat to low, cover, and simmer about 30 minutes.

3. Serve hot over El Arroz Blanco Mas Sabroso—The Ultimate White Rice (page 170). And, yes, if you're feeling Italian, you can even serve this dish with pasta!

Glenn: *Arroz con Pollo is enjoyed by many Latin cultures. The Cuban version features rich and subtle flavors. It's a favorite Cuban Sunday lunch dish.*

Jorge: *Some Cuban versions of Arroz con Pollo use wine and some use beer. But we believe the use of beer is more typical and tastes better!*

Raúl: *This recipe is loved by everyone!*

Jorge: *In fact, this recipe had its origin in a recipe sent to us by an American lady who had fond memories of Cuban meals with her friend's family.*

Glenn: *The Three Guys have done some tinkering with this recipe over the years. We've made a few changes here and there and we think it tastes better than ever!*

Arroz con Pollo
Chicken with Rice

. . . .

INGREDIENTS

Serves 6 to 8

5	strips of bacon
8	chicken thighs, bone in, skin on
	Salt, pepper, and ground cumin
	Olive oil for sautéing
2	cups chopped white onion
2	cups chopped green pepper
4	cloves garlic, mashed
3½	cups chicken broth
1	(12-ounce) bottle of beer
1	(8-ounce) can of tomato sauce
1	teaspoon Bijol powder
1	bay leaf
2	teaspoons oregano
2	teaspoons ground cumin
1½	teaspoons salt
½	teaspoon black pepper
3½	cups parboiled rice
½	cup frozen baby green peas

1. Sauté the bacon in a large frying pan. Reduce heat to low and let the fat render out of the bacon—about 10 minutes. Meanwhile, season the chicken lightly with salt, pepper, and a little cumin. Once the fat is released, remove the bacon, increase temperature to medium-high and add the chicken to the hot bacon fat. Remove the chicken when it is browned on both sides.

2. Add a little olive oil to the same pan you fried the chicken in, and sauté the onion and green pepper until the onion is translucent. Add the mashed garlic and cook an additional 1 to 2 minutes, stirring frequently.

3. Pour the chicken broth and beer into a large covered pot. Add the browned chicken pieces, cooked onion and green pepper, tomato sauce, Bijol, bay leaf, oregano, cumin, salt, and pepper. And, hey, why let all that delicious bacon go to waste? Chop it up and toss it in! Stir in the rice. Bring to a boil. When the rice has absorbed some of the liquid, reduce heat to low, cover and simmer for about 30 to 45 minutes, or until the rice is fully cooked and not soupy. Finally, toss in the frozen peas and cook for an additional 5 minutes only.

4. For a dinner, serve the whole chicken pieces with the rice. For a party, you may remove the chicken; skin, debone, and break it into bite-size chunks. However, please DON'T try to substitute any boneless, skinless chicken in this recipe— unless you enjoy serving a disaster!

Jorge: *Don't confuse Bistec Empanizado with those chicken fried steaks you've probably had elsewhere. This is NOT a deep-fried piece of ground beef!*

Raúl: *The secret to this one is a light coating of cracker crumbs.*

Glenn: *Make sure you grind the crackers in a food processor to a fine consistency.*

Jorge: *They can be Cuban crackers, saltines, and so on. We especially like Keebler Club Crackers, the ones with the little Cuban elves on the box.*

Glenn: *They give the dish a nice buttery flavor.*

Bistec Empanizado
Cuban Breaded Steak

. . . .

INGREDIENTS

Serves 4

¼	cup olive oil
½	cup sour orange juice
2	tablespoons vinegar
1	cup finely chopped onion
1½	pounds sirloin steak (about 6 ounces per serving)
1	cup cracker meal (finely ground crackers)
2	teaspoons garlic powder
½	teaspoon salt
2	egg whites, beaten
	Olive oil for sautéing
	Fresh cilantro, chopped
	Freshly ground black pepper

1. Mix olive oil, sour orange juice, vinegar, and chopped onion to make a mojo marinade. Add un-pounded beef steaks, cover, and marinate for 20 minutes. Remove steaks from marinade and place them, one at a time, between two pieces of waxed paper. Using a meat mallet, pound steaks to ¼-inch thickness. (This also helps infuse the meat with the marinade.) Return steaks to marinade.

2. If you are in a hurry, proceed with the remaining steps. Otherwise, refrigerate and continue marinating for 1 to 4 hours. Remove beef, save marinade.

3. In a medium bowl, combine cracker meal, garlic powder, and salt. Dip wet beef in egg whites, then dip in cracker mixture, coating well on both sides. Sauté to desired doneness in olive oil. (We like ours rare!) Remove from pan and place on plate. Use some of the reserved marinade (with the onions!) to deglaze the frying pan: cook at high heat, stirring constantly until onions are cooked and the sauce reduces somewhat. Pour sauce over steaks and sprinkle with chopped cilantro and freshly ground black pepper.

SOUR ORANGE JUICE

*W*HEREVER A RECIPE *calls for sour orange juice, the orange in question is* NOT *one that has been left out of the refrigerator too long! The sour orange (sometimes called bitter orange, or* naranja agria*) used in Cuban cooking tastes that way right off the tree. The seeds for many sour orange trees growing in Miami today were smuggled out of Cuba by many exiles over the years.*

If you can't get sour orange juice in your area, you can make this substitution in ALL *recipes:*

> *2 parts orange juice*
> *1 part lemon juice*
> *1 part lime juice*

This is about as close as you can get to the real thing. You may also order bottled sour orange juice from several companies; please see Sources (page 224) for complete details.

Jorge: *This is the most typical steak served in Cuban restaurants. If your butcher hails from Havana, you've got it made!*

Raúl: *He'll know exactly what you're looking for!*

Glenn: *Otherwise talk to your local butcher and get him or her to slice sirloin steak about ¼ inch thick.*

Bistec de Palomilla

Palomilla Steak

. . . .

INGREDIENTS

Serves 4

4 (8-ounce) boneless sirloin steaks, slice thin
  Olive oil for frying
  Juice of 1 lime
4 tablespoons butter
3 cloves garlic, peeled and minced
  Salt and freshly ground black pepper to taste

1. Place steaks between two sheets of waxed paper and use a meat hammer to pound them very thin. Be sure to do this on a cutting board or other suitable pounding surface, thus avoiding those embarrassing and marriage-threatening hammer marks in the countertop!

2. Heat olive oil over high heat in a large frying pan. Just before the oil starts to smoke, drop the steaks in, 1 or 2 at a time. You have to be very quick! Heat each side no more than 1 minute—less time if you like your meat rare. Remove the steaks once they are cooked to your satisfaction and put them someplace where they can stay hot and avoid attracting the attention of your family dog, the neighbor's dog, or worse yet, the neighbor.

3. Remove pan from heat and quickly add lime juice to deglaze the pan. Add butter and garlic. Return to low heat and cook long enough to heat through, but do not brown or otherwise overcook the garlic. Pour sauce over the steaks, season with salt and pepper, and serve with fresh lime sections.

DOMINO PARK
Jorge gets ready for a game of dominos at Maximo Gomez park in Little Havana.

Raúl: *It seems like every culture has its own version of the pot roast.*

Glenn: *It's a great way to turn a lesser cut of meat into a delicious feast— moist and tender!*

Raúl: *This Cuban version gets its flavor from the chorizo and green olives. Seven cloves of garlic may seem like a lot, but we're not making ice cream.*

Jorge: *The garlic infuses the meat with such a wonderful flavor!*

Glenn: *This dish also confers temporary immunity against Cuban vampires.*

Boliche
Cuban Pot Roast

. . . .

INGREDIENTS

Serves 6 to 8

6	links Spanish chorizo
3 to 4	pounds chuck or rump roast
7	cloves garlic, mashed
1	teaspoon salt
½	teaspoon pepper
	Flour
½	cup olive oil
1	(14½-ounce) can diced tomatoes
1	bay leaf
1	tablespoon oregano
4	medium potatoes, quartered
1	large onion, sliced
¼	cup green olives
1	cup water
½	cup red wine

1. Remove the casings from the chorizo. Cut a slit in the beef and insert the chorizo and some of the garlic inside. Salt, pepper, and lightly flour the roast; brown on all sides in a frying pan with the olive oil. Place all ingredients except the water and wine (including the roast and the oil you browned it in) in a large covered pot or Dutch oven with the potatoes, onion slices, and green olives on top.

2. Mix the water and the wine. Add just enough of this mixture to cover the bottom 2 inches of the pan. Bring to a boil, reduce heat to low and simmer partially covered (leave your lid slightly ajar to let some of the steam escape) for approximately 3 to 4 hours. Check the roast occasionally and add the water/wine mixture as necessary. When the roast is fork-tender, remove it from the pot. Remove bay leaf and discard.

3. Arrange meat and potatoes on a large serving platter. Garnish the plate with the cooked onion slices and green olives. Slice beef at the table.

FOLK ART
A Havana bus by
Cookie of Calle Ocho.

Jorge: *Some Irish people we know always brag about their delicious Irish stew! However, we Cubans have our own version.*

Raúl: *What makes it different? Well, unlike the Irish, we're not afraid to use spices!*

Jorge: *Green olives, raisins, and capers give this stew its distinctive taste.*

Glenn: *Our suggestion? Cook some up and serve it on St. Patrick's Day to all of your Irish friends.*

Carne Guisado

Cuban Beef Stew

. . . .

INGREDIENTS

Serves 6

4	tablespoons olive oil
2	cups chopped onion
2	cups chopped green pepper
6	cloves garlic, mashed
2	pounds lean beef, sirloin tip or round, cut in cubes
	White flour for dredging
2	teaspoons ground cumin
2	teaspoons dried oregano
1	teaspoon salt
½	teaspoon black pepper
1	cup red wine
1	(15-ounce) can tomato sauce
3	tablespoons vinegar
¼	cup stuffed green olives
¼	cup raisins
2	tablespoons capers
2	bay leaves

1½ to 2	cups water
4 to 5	potatoes, peeled and cut into large chunks
	Salt and pepper to taste

1. Heat oil over medium heat in a large sauté pan. Add onion and pepper; cook and stir until transparent. Add garlic and sauté for an additional minute.

2. Lightly salt and pepper the meat cubes and dredge in flour. Add the meat to the pan and brown on all sides. Add the cumin, oregano, salt, and pepper and cook for 3 minutes. Add wine, tomato sauce, vinegar, olives, raisins, capers, and bay leaves. Add just enough water to cover the meat. Bring to a boil, reduce heat to low, cover, and simmer until fork-tender, about 1 to 2 hours. Add more water if the stew becomes too thick.

3. Add potatoes and cook, covered, until potatoes are tender. Season with salt and pepper to taste. Serve hot with Pan Cubano—Cuban Bread (page 182) or crackers.

Jorge: *This is the dish we made for Keith Famie of the Food Network when he came to Miami.*

Glenn: *In Argentina, where this style of cooking developed, churrasco actually refers to many types of meats prepared on the grill.*

Raúl: *But here in Miami,* churrasco *specifically refers to a cut of beef prepared in the Argentine style.*

Jorge: *It's also popular with Nicaraguans. You'll see it on the menu of many restaurants. The* churrasco *is a long flat cut of skirt steak, cut from the "plate" of the cow.*

Glenn: *You might find it sold at some butcher shops as a "plate" steak. Don't confuse it with the flank steak, a similar cut, but* NOT *the same!*

Jorge: *The* churrasco *is typically marinated to make it tender and full of flavor. The Argentine version uses a mildly flavored marinade or sometimes no marinade at all.*

Churrasco Estilo Cubano
Cuban-Style Skirt Steak

. . . .

INGREDIENTS

Servings are based on the amount of meat. Allow ¾ to 1 pound per person, depending on side dishes.

Cuban Mojo Marinade for Churrasco

2	heads garlic, about 20 to 30 cloves
2	teaspoons salt
1	teaspoon black peppercorns
1 1/2	cups sour orange juice (see page 109)
1/2	cup minced onion
2	teaspoons oregano
1	cup Spanish olive oil

Beef skirt steak cut in long steaks
(about ¾ pound or more per person)

1. Using a mortar and pestle, mash garlic, salt, and peppercorns into a paste. Stir in sour orange juice, onion, and oregano. Let sit at room temperature for 30 minutes. Heat the olive oil in a 2 quart saucepan until hot, but NOT deep-frying hot! We're looking for something in the neighborhood of 220 degrees F. Remove the oil from heat and quickly whisk in the garlic-orange juice mixture until well blended. Let cool before using as a marinade.

2. Place the meat in a large bowl or pan. Add enough cooled Mojo to cover the meat. Place a cover over the bowl or pan and place in the refrigerator a minimum of 5 hours, preferably overnight.

3. Grill the marinated steaks outdoors on the barbecue. Make sure your grill is ready. Gas grills need to be preheated until the grill surface is very hot. In a barbecue grill, the coals need to be white hot. You can cook churrasco however you like your steak—from rare to well done. However, the rarer the meat, the more tender and flavorful. Remember, thin steaks cook very quickly on a hot grill, so remain in the standby position at grill side, meat fork in the upright and ready position! Note that this position does leave one hand free for a Cuban beer or your choice of other liquid refreshment!

4. Serve the meat with Chimichurri (page 168)—it tastes great!

Glenn: *We like to "Cubanize" the dish by marinating the meat overnight in our own homemade Mojo marinade.*

Raúl: Churrasco *is always served with a good Chimichurri sauce. We like to use our Cuban version—it is much more flavorful than the typical Argentine version!*

Jorge: *If you're having trouble finding churrasco-cut beef in your area, you might try a Latin American or even a Mexican market. Mexican cooks like to use this cut of meat for making fajitas. Otherwise, talk to a good butcher. Tell them you want a skirt steak, cut from the plate and sliced long.*

Jorge: *A chef in Chicago contacted us several years ago and wanted to know if we had a recipe for Cuban lamb shanks.*

Glenn: *Although we had eaten this dish several times over the years at various Miami restaurants, we'd never made it ourselves.*

Raúl: *But we asked around, got several good suggestions, and came up with our own very good recipe!*

Jorge: *Then our friend in Chicago (a professionally trained chef) surprised us by adapting our recipe to his own lamb-cooking methods.*

Glenn: *Our friend works at a restaurant that NEVER shares its recipes, so he will remain anonymous. If you ever eat at one of the major hotels in Chicago, you might get a chance to taste some of his great cooking!*

Cordero en Salsa de Vino Rojo

Lamb Shanks in Red Wine Sauce

. . . .

INGREDIENTS

Serves 4

3	pounds lamb shanks, cut in 1½-inch pieces
	Salt, pepper, cumin, paprika for seasoning lamb
	Flour for dredging
	Olive oil for frying
1	cup red wine
1	cup chicken stock
½	cup tomato sauce
1	teaspoon oregano
1	teaspoon cumin
¼	cup olive oil
1	teaspoon Bijol powder
2	cups chopped white onion
3	carrots, diced
5	cloves garlic, mashed

1. Preheat oven to 275 degrees F.

2. Generously season lamb shanks with salt, pepper, cumin, and paprika. Dredge the seasoned lamb shanks in flour. Brown the meat in a frying pan with a little olive oil.

3. Mix wine, chicken stock, tomato sauce, oregano, cumin, olive oil, and Bijol in a small bowl. Place the lamb shanks, onion, carrot, and garlic in a covered kettle (suitable for use in the oven). Pour the wine sauce over the meat and vegetables. Liquid should only come up about halfway on the meat.

4. Cover the kettle and let the lamb shanks braise in the oven for 1½ hours. (Add more sauce if needed to keep the correct level.) Turn the shanks, cover, and cook for another 1½ hours, or until the meat is fork-tender.

5. Carefully remove the shanks from the pot and keep warm. Reduce the sauce slightly by bringing to a boil and cooking off some of the water. Serve the shanks over El Arroz Blanco Más Sabroso—The Ultimate White Rice (page 170) with the reduced sauce poured on top. As Martha Stewart might say, "at table, maintain proper decorum." In other words, please don't make any wisecracks, as Jorge has, about Mary OR her little lamb—it upsets the kids.

Jorge: *When we don't have the time …*

Raúl: *… or enough hungry Cubans around …*

Jorge: *… to roast a whole pig, we make our Lechón Asado using a fresh bone-in ham.*

Glenn: *Many butchers in other parts of the United States call this a "green" ham. Just make sure you ask for un-smoked or unprocessed ham with the skin still on.*

Raúl: *That's the most important part—you need the skin and the layer of fat underneath.*

Jorge: *You can cook your lechón in the oven or outside on the grill. A covered grill (such as the Weber kettle) where you can bank the coals to the side, leaving an empty space beneath your ham, works best.*

Glenn: *I've had good luck with a three-burner gas grill. Just turn off the middle burner and adjust the front and back burners to keep the grill at the right temperature.*

Lechón Asado

Roast Pork

. . . .

INGREDIENTS

Servings are based on the size of the ham. Allow ¼ to ½ pound per person, (portion sizes may vary depending on the size of the persons involved, degree of hunger, and the number of side dishes).

1   bone-in fresh ham with skin on
     (or have your butcher butterfly it for you)

     Mojo (page 178), enough for marinating and roasting

120

1. To marinate, pierce pork as many times as you can with a sharp knife or fork. Pour Mojo over pork, cover, and let sit in refrigerator at least 2 to 3 hours or preferably overnight.

2. Select one of three different cooking methods:

   A. To roast in the oven, preheat oven to 450 degrees F. Place the pork, fattest side up, in an open roasting pan. Place pan in oven and reduce temperature to 325 degrees F. Occasionally spoon extra Mojo over the roast as it cooks. Remove roast from oven when the internal temperature reaches 155 degrees F on a meat thermometer. Immediately cover with foil and let rest for 10 minutes before slicing and serving. The roast will continue to cook after you remove it from the heat. A perfectly cooked pork roast will be slightly pink to pale white in the middle and the juices will run clear.

   B. To grill on the barbecue, use a covered grill such as the Weber kettle or a covered gas grill. Bank the coals to each side of the covered grill, leaving an empty space beneath your ham. If using a gas grill, use front and rear burners only. The idea is to cook with indirect heat. Spoon extra Mojo over the roast occasionally as it cooks. If not using a gas grill, add charcoal to the sides as needed to maintain roasting temperature. Remove roast from the barbecue when the internal temperature reaches 155 degrees F on a meat thermometer. Immediately cover with foil and let rest for 10 minutes before slicing and serving. The roast will continue to cook after you remove it from the heat. A perfectly cooked pork roast will be slightly pink to pale white in the middle and the juices will run clear.

   C. To cook on the stovetop, place ham in a large Dutch oven or a covered stock pan—whatever you have that the pork will fit in. Add about 1 cup of Mojo to the pan. Bring to a boil. Adjust the heat to low, cover, and cook until completely done. Add marinade as needed to keep at least 1 inch of liquid in bottom of pan; otherwise the roast will burn.

Raúl: *You also can make this on top of the stove in a large Dutch oven. Adjust the heat to low, cover, and cook until completely done.*

Jorge: *My sister, Esther, usually adds a fresh ham or two when we do our pig roasts, just to make sure there's plenty of* lechón *for everyone!*

Raúl: *If you've been to a Cuban sandwich window, a Cuban bakery, or many Miami restaurants, you may have seen a stack of browned meat sitting under a heating lamp.*

Jorge: *The meat is pork, and there is a dish prepared in the same way called Masitas de Puerco Fritas.*

Raúl: *In Mexican markets, they sell something very similar called carnitas.*

Glenn: *The meat makes a delicious sandwich with Cuban bread. Or eat it straight with recommended side dishes.*

Masitas de Puerco Fritas

Fried Pork Chunks

. . . .

INGREDIENTS

Serves 4 to 6

2½	pounds pork loin or boneless country-style ribs
	Mojo (page 178)
2	cups water
½	teaspoon salt
¼	cup lard
½	onion, sliced into rings
	Lime wedges

1. Cut pork into 2-inch chunks. Cover the chunks with Mojo. Marinate for at least 4 hours or overnight in the refrigerator.

2. Remove meat from marinade and pat dry with a paper towel. Place the meat in a pot with water, salt, and lard. Bring to a boil, reduce heat to low, and simmer, uncovered, until all water boils away—about 30 to 45 minutes. Don't, as we have, take this opportunity to walk the dog, mow the lawn, or shoot the breeze with the next-door neighbor. You must remain alert and vigilant. The time between when the water boils away and the whole pan of meat is turned into charcoal is very short!

3. Lightly brown the cooked pork in the melted fat until crispy on the outside—you don't want to overcook it! Toss in the onion slices and sauté briefly. Garnish with lime wedges.

4. Serve with Plátanos Maduros—Fried Sweet Plantains (page 190), Moros y Cristianos—Moors and Christians (page 180), and El Arroz Blanco Más Sabroso —The Ultimate White Rice (page 170).

Jorge: *A picadillo is a type of hash. Picadillo literally means "minced meat." However, in Cuba it's a dish made with onions, green pepper, tomatoes, and spices.*

Glenn: *In a Cuban household, Picadillo is the equivalent of several American home-style favorites: sloppy Joes, Hamburger Helper, and homemade spaghetti—all things that a mom can prepare simply and inexpensively for her family.*

Jorge: *Picadillo will never be considered a gourmet dish.*

Raúl: *But never mind, I love it! It's great served over rice with a side of fried green plantains!*

Picadillo

Cuban-Style Hash

. . . .

INGREDIENTS

Serves 8

2	cups diced onion
2	cups seeded and finely chopped green bell pepper
	Olive oil for sautéing
4	cloves garlic, minced
2	pounds ground beef or ground round
3	tomatoes, peeled, seeded, and chopped
1	teaspoon ground cumin
¼	teaspoon cinnamon
⅛	teaspoon ground cloves
1	teaspoon oregano
½	cup chopped green olives
⅓	cup raisins
	Salt and pepper to taste

1. Sauté onion and green pepper in olive oil in a large frying pan. Sauté about 5 minutes, until the onion is softened, and then add the garlic and ground beef. Mash the onion and green pepper into the sautéing meat and cook until the meat is browned, about 5 minutes. Add the tomatoes, cumin, cinnamon, cloves, and oregano. Reduce heat to low, cover and simmer for about 15 minutes. Add olives and raisins and simmer 5 minutes longer. Salt and pepper to taste.

2. Serve hot over El Arroz Blanco Más Sabroso—The Ultimate White Rice (page 170); include fresh Tostones—Fried Green Plantain (page 194) for a special treat that will engender the gratitude of small children!

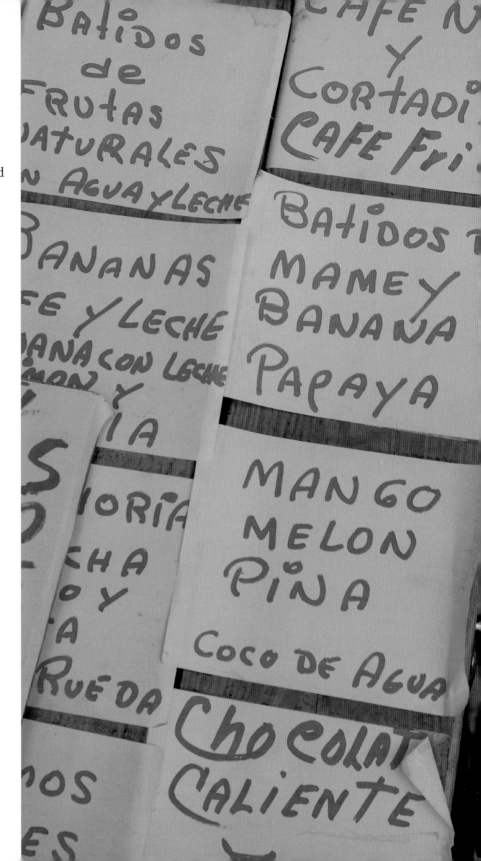

Jorge: *Confession time: Cubans eat a lot of rice. There I said it, and I'm glad I got that off of my chest. I love my rice and I'm proud of it!*

Glenn: *Do Cubans ever get sick of all that rice? Not in the annals of recorded history!*

Raúl: *There are times when we don't have rice on the table.*

Jorge: *I'm thinking hurricane—the last time we ran out of rice at our house!*

Glenn: *However, there are a few dishes that ARE NOT served with rice. This is a nice picadillo recipe that has the starch built in, so rice is not necessary. That's right, rice is NOT necessary in this dish!*

Jorge: *I think I'm going to cry…*

Picadillo con Papas

Picadillo with Potatoes

. . . .

INGREDIENTS

Serves 8

3	cups peeled and diced potatoes
	Olive oil for sautéing
2	cups chopped onion
2	cups diced green pepper
2	pounds ground beef or ground round
6	small Roma tomatoes, chopped
4	cloves garlic, minced
¼	cup chopped green olives
¼	cup vinegar
½	cup red wine
1	teaspoon salt
¼	teaspoon black pepper

1. Sauté potatoes in olive oil until lightly brown and set aside. Sauté onion and green pepper in olive oil. Add the ground beef, chopped tomatoes, and garlic. Cook uncovered until the beef is browned, stirring frequently. Add the potatoes, green olives, vinegar, wine, salt, and black pepper to the beef mixture. Cover and simmer about 30 minutes, or until potatoes are tender.

2. Serve hot. Without rice. That's right—WITHOUT rice! (Would someone please pick Raúl up off of the floor?)

Jorge: *Here's a great way to roast a chicken.*

Glenn: *The key is to give your chicken a split personality. A meat cleaver usually does the trick.*

Jorge: *Just split the chicken down the middle of the backbone and through the breast.*

Raúl: *This is a very good chicken; it is always moist and very flavorful.*

Glenn: *If you don't like garlic, you had better stay away from this one.*

Raúl: *Hey, if you don't like garlic, you had better stay away from Cuban food!*

Pollo Asado al Ajillo

Garlic Roasted Chicken

. . . .

INGREDIENTS

Serves 4

2	cups quartered onion
10	cloves garlic mashed with 1 teaspoon salt
½	cup white wine
¼	cup olive oil
2	teaspoons white vinegar
1	(3-pound) frying chicken, cut in half
¼	cup lime juice
½	teaspoon black pepper
2	teaspoons ground cumin
	Flour for dusting
	Olive oil for frying

1. Place the onion, half of the garlic/salt mixture, wine, olive oil, and vinegar in a blender and chop thoroughly. Pour marinade over the chicken and refrigerate, covered, for 2 to 4 hours. Drain marinade from chicken and pat chicken dry with a paper towel.

2. Preheat oven to 375 degrees F.

3. Rub the chicken halves on both sides with the rest of the mashed garlic/salt mixture. If you can get some of this underneath the skin without ripping, great. Sprinkle the chicken with lime juice and then black pepper and cumin on both sides. Dust chicken lightly with flour and brown chicken quickly on both sides in olive oil in a sauté pan.

4. Place chicken halves in a roasting pan, skin side up. Roast 30 to 45 minutes, or until juices run clear. Use a meat thermometer if you need to, or if your "significant other" gave you one for Christmas.

Jorge: *Many people don't realize that there are a lot of Cubans of Chinese descent. The Chinese have also influenced Cuban cuisine, giving us fried rice and several types of stir-fry.*

Raúl: *This recipe is for a sweet and spicy chicken stir-fry.*

Glenn: *Make sure your mangoes are very ripe! They should be easy to slice.*

Jorge: *If you're like Raúl or me, and it's summer, you can just walk out to your backyard and pick a few fresh mangoes right off the tree.*

Raúl: *If not, make a trip to your local grocer. Most carry mangoes all year-round—the off-season mangoes come from Mexico and Central America.*

Pollo Agridulce

Sweet and Spicy Chicken

. . . .

INGREDIENTS

Serves 4

3	tablespoons olive oil
3	tablespoons butter
2	cups chopped onion
5	cloves garlic mashed with ½ teaspoon salt
1½	pounds chicken thighs, skinned, deboned, and cut into bite-size pieces
¼	cup brown sugar
1	cup ripe mango chunks
1	teaspoon ground ginger
1	teaspoon ground cumin
⅛	teaspoon red pepper flakes
½	cup chopped fresh cilantro

1. Heat the oil and butter over medium heat in a large skillet. Sauté the onion until translucent. Add garlic and chicken and continue sautéing, stirring constantly, until the chicken is lightly browned.

2. Add the brown sugar, mango, ginger, cumin, and red pepper flakes. Cover and simmer over medium-low heat until the chicken is cooked through, approximately 5 to 10 minutes. Toss in the cilantro during the last minute or two.

3. Serve hot over El Arroz Blanco Más Sabroso—The Ultimate White Rice (page 170).

Jorge: *"Medical experts" have also told us that marinades are the way to go when grilling.*

Raúl: *We can't make any medical claims ourselves, but we guess we'll take their word for it.*

Glenn: *Supposedly the marinade process removes many of the nasty things that can be created during the grilling process. So marinated meat on the grill is healthier for you!*

Jorge: *At least that's what they tell us …*

Glenn: *… and who are we to argue?*

Raúl: *One thing is certain. Medical experts agree that this chicken is very tasty!*

Pollo de Guayaba Dulce
Sweet Guava Chicken

. . . .

INGREDIENTS

Serves 4

	Juice of 2 medium limes
¼	cup olive oil
1	tablespoon ground cumin
½	teaspoon salt
⅛	teaspoon pepper
4	cloves garlic, mashed
1	(3-pound) chicken, cut-up

Salt, pepper, and cumin for seasoning

Glaze

¼	cup guava jelly
¼	cup apple juice
¼	cup fresh lemon juice
¼	cup brown sugar

1. Mix lime juice, olive oil, cumin, salt, pepper, and garlic together. Pour over chicken in a shallow baking dish. A Ziploc freezer bag works great, too, and allows you to force out the air and coat the chicken with marinade. Cover the chicken and refrigerate for at least 3 hours, preferably overnight.

2. Discard marinade. Pat chicken dry with a paper towel. Season the chicken with additional salt, pepper, and a little cumin.

3. Fire up the burners on a gas grill or light charcoal briquettes to preheat the grilling surface. Grill the chicken over medium heat. (Try to use the indirect heating method if you have a Weber grill or equivalent. This will avoid those oh-so-nasty flare-ups.) Cook for approximately 30 minutes, turning occasionally until chicken begins to brown.

4. For the glaze, mix guava jelly, apple juice, lemon juice, and brown sugar in a 1-quart saucepan and bring to a boil. Reduce heat to low and simmer, uncovered, stirring frequently, until glaze thickens and reduces somewhat, about 5 to 10 minutes. Remove from heat.

5. Brush chicken with glaze mixture frequently during the last 15 minutes of cooking. Once glazed, keep a close eye on the chicken because sugar burns easily and tastes terrible. (Just take our word for it on this one!) Chicken is done when the juices run clear (or just clandestinely slice into one of the larger pieces to make sure there are no traces of pink). A meat thermometer is also a handy accessory for the faint of heart!

Raúl: *Several readers have asked, "Hey, Raúl! Where do I buy oxtail?"*

Jorge: *You don't see that many oxen in the United States. In fact, when was the last time you saw one?*

Glenn: *So how could there possibly be enough oxtails to go around?*

Raúl: *The oxtails eaten in the United States actually come from a cow. Oxtail is skinned and usually sold cut in pieces. Obviously, the tail of a cow has a lot of bone! However, the meat, when slow cooked, is very tender and delicious!*

Glenn: *I just have one question.*

Raúl: *What's that?*

Glenn: *Why don't they just call it Cow Tail Stew?*

Rabo Encendido
Oxtail Stew

• • • • • • • • • • • • • • • •

INGREDIENTS

Serves 6

4	pounds oxtail, disjointed
½	cup olive oil
½	cup red wine
1	teaspoon salt
	Flour for coating meat
	Olive oil for frying
2½	cups bite-size onion chunks
2½	cups bite-size green pepper chunks
2	cups bite-size red pepper chunks
1	cup diced carrots
1	cup diced potatoes
3	cloves garlic mashed with ½ teaspoon salt
1	teaspoon Sazón Accent
½	teaspoon ground allspice
1	teaspoon nutmeg

1   bay leaf

1   (15-ounce) can tomato sauce

1   cup red wine

2½ cups beef broth

1. Marinate the meat in a mixture of olive oil, red wine, and salt at least 4 hours or preferably overnight. Drain marinade and discard.

2. Lightly coat meat with flour. Brown meat on both sides in oil. Remove meat and add onion, peppers, carrots, and potatoes. Sauté until the potatoes brown and the onions are translucent. Add garlic/salt mixture and continue cooking for another minute or so. Add remaining ingredients, including the meat. Bring to a boil, reduce heat to low, cover, and simmer until the meat is fork-tender, about 1½ to 2 hours. Remove bay leaf.

3. Serve everything hot over El Arroz Blanco Más Sabroso—The Ultimate White Rice (page 170).

Raúl: *The name of this dish in Spanish is "Old Clothes."*

Jorge: *It's probably called that because the meat gets stringy and frayed.*

Glenn: *Which looks a lot like Raúl's "lucky" fishing shirt, the one his wife, Esther, finally threw out one day when he wasn't looking!*

Raúl: *Hey, I caught many fish with that shirt!*

Ropa Vieja
Shredded Beef

. . . .

INGREDIENTS

Serves 8

4	pounds chuck or arm roast, well marbled
	Salt and pepper for seasoning
	Flour for dusting
	Olive oil for browning
	Water
1	green pepper, chunked
1	onion sliced
5	cloves garlic, chopped
2	cups white onion, chopped
4	cloves garlic mashed with 1 teaspoon salt
2	cups green pepper, chopped
	Olive oil for sautéing
4	ounces tomato paste
1	(32-ounce) can crushed tomatoes
2	tablespoons ground cumin
1	cup red wine
1	bay leaf
	Salt and pepper to taste

1. Do not trim excess fat from meat before cooking. (You can remove the fat when you shred the beef.) Salt and pepper the meat and dust lightly with flour.

2. Brown the meat in oil in a large Dutch oven. Add enough water to surround the meat, but NOT cover it. Add green pepper, onion, and garlic. Simmer, covered, until meat is fork-tender, about 2 hours. (Add more water as necessary to keep from burning!) Remove from heat and cool. Discard vegetables. Shred the meat.

3. In the same pan you cooked the meat in, sauté onions, garlic, and green pepper in oil until limp. Add tomato paste, crushed tomatoes, cumin, wine, and bay leaf. Salt and pepper to taste. Finally, add the shredded beef. Cover and cook on low for about 30 minutes, stirring occasionally. Remove bay leaf.

4. Serve with El Arroz Blanco Más Sabroso— The Ultimate White Rice (page 170).

Glenn: *This is one of Raúl's favorites!!*

Raúl: *Tasajo is dried beef that's been reconstituted by soaking in water. It's then lightly sautéed until crispy.*

Glenn: *You can also serve Tasajo with a Salsa Criolla—Creole Sauce.*

Jorge: *Raúl likes his served plain with black beans and white rice.*

Raúl: *Once you try it, you'll love it!*

Tasajo
Dried Beef

· ·

INGREDIENTS

Serves 4

  2 pounds dried beef tasajo—available in Latin markets
     Water
  ¼ cup sour orange juice (see page 109)
  5 cloves garlic, mashed
2½ cups sliced onion
  1 teaspoon oregano
  ½ cup olive oil

1. Cut the dried beef into large but manageable chunks. Place in a pan with enough water to cover. Soak the meat in the refrigerator overnight. Drain.

Tip: Many people peel and quarter a raw potato and add it to the soaking tasajo. The potato draws off some of the salt from the water.

2. Cover beef with water in a 3-quart saucepan. Bring to a boil, reduce heat to low, and simmer for 1 hour. Drain. Cover the beef once again with water, bring to a boil, reduce heat to low, and simmer until the meat is soft enough to separate into strands. Drain.

3. Pound the meat out slightly with a meat hammer until it shreds. Season the meat by sprinkling with a little sour orange juice. Sauté garlic, onion, and oregano in olive oil until onion begins to go limp. Remove the onion and set aside. Sauté the shredded beef in the same oil until the meat is brown and crisp.

4. Serve with cooked onion on the side. Also try Salsa Criolla—Creole Sauce (page 182), Frijoles Negros—Black Beans (page 172), El Arroz Blanco Más Sabroso—The Ultimate White Rice (page 170) as accompaniments.

Glenn: *We generally make our Vaca Frita with leftover pot roast. It's a Cuban tradition to always make more than enough food.*

Raúl: *No one leaves the table hungry in a Cuban house! There are always plenty of leftovers.*

Jorge: *If you don't have any leftover roast, you can also start from scratch by taking a chuck roast and cooking it in a covered pan on low heat on the stovetop.*

Glenn: *Just use the freshly cooked roast recipe on the facing page.*

Vaca Frita

Fried Beef

. . . .

INGREDIENTS

Serves 4 to 6

1½	pounds leftover beef roast
3	tablespoons dry sherry
	Salt and pepper to taste
1	teaspoon oregano
1	teaspoon cumin
5	garlic cloves, chopped fine
2½	cups sliced yellow onion
2	cups cored and sliced green bell pepper
	Olive oil for sautéing
	Juice of ½ lime
	Lime wedges

1. Pound the meat with a meat hammer or rolling pin to break into strands. Sprinkle meat with a little sherry and season with salt, pepper, oregano, and cumin.

2. Sauté the garlic cloves, onion, and green pepper in the oil until the onion begins to go limp. Then add the meat. Continue sautéing until the meat is hot and somewhat crispy. Squeeze the lime juice over the meat. Garnish with lime wedges.

Roast Recipe for Vaca Frita

INGREDIENTS

1	(3-pound) chuck or arm roast
	Salt and pepper for seasoning
	Flour for dusting
	Olive oil for browning
½	cup red wine
	Water
1	whole bay leaf
2	cups sliced white onion
2	stalks celery, chopped
1	teaspoon whole black peppercorns

1. Salt and pepper the roast. Dust the roast lightly with flour and brown on both sides in olive oil.

2. Place the roast in a covered pan or Dutch oven. Add the wine and just enough water to surround the roast but NOT cover. Add bay leaf, onion, celery, and black peppercorns to season. Check frequently and add more water as needed. The roast is done when the meat is tender and starts to shred—approximately 30 to 45 minutes per pound. Discard all vegetables and bay leaf. Use meat in the Vaca Frita recipe above.

PAELLA CUBANA
Three Guys add a little zing to traditional Cuban-Style Paella. There's seafood in every bite! (Recipe page 150.)

Seafood

Raúl: *In Castro's Cuba, unless you lived on the coast or were a fisherman by trade, you didn't get to eat a lot of fish. It just wasn't available.*

Glenn: *Yet Cubans have always had a passion for seafood. In the United States, Cuban Americans finally found access to all of the seafood they could ever hope for.*

Jorge: *Lobster, crab, and shrimp are big favorites.*

Raúl: *This Cuban classic blends the delicious flavor of yellow rice with the delicate taste of shrimp. Don't overcook the shrimp!*

Camarones y Arroz Amarillo

Shrimp and Yellow Rice

. . . .

INGREDIENTS

Serves 6

2	pounds large shrimp, peeled, deveined, and butterflied (save shells)
4	cups water
½	teaspoon salt
2	cups diced white onion
1½	cups diced red bell pepper
1½	cups diced green bell pepper
¼	cup olive oil
4	garlic cloves, crushed and chopped fine
3	cups shrimp broth (see instructions)
3	cups chicken broth
3	cups uncooked rice
1	(14-ounce) can tomatoes, chopped
1	teaspoon Bijol powder
1½	teaspoons salt
¼	teaspoon pepper
6	strips bacon, diced
	Salt, pepper, and ground cumin for seasoning shrimp
⅔	cup frozen green peas

144

1. Make a broth of the reserved shrimp shells by placing them in a 3-quart saucepan with approximately 1 quart of water and ½ teaspoon of salt. Bring to a boil, reduce heat to low, and simmer, uncovered, for about 10 minutes.

2. In a large sauté pan, sauté the onion, red pepper, and green pepper in olive oil until the onion is translucent. Add the chopped garlic and cook an additional minute, stirring frequently.

3. Remove the simmering shrimp shells from the heat and strain out all of the shells. Take 3 cups of this shrimp broth and pour into a large covered pot. Add chicken broth, the cooked onion and pepper, the rice, tomatoes, Bijol, salt, and pepper. Bring to a boil, reduce heat to low, cover, and simmer until rice is fully cooked and most of the liquid has been absorbed—about 30 to 45 minutes.

4. Now, this is an important step. Find something else to do for about 20 minutes or so. Let the dog out, clean your boat, order some Cuban food ingredients online, or catch up on your reading. The important thing is to do something productive. We bet you're thinking a nap would be great right now. Think again. Unless you have a very reliable alarm clock or someone else to watch the rice, forget it.

5. By the time you return to the kitchen the rice is well on its way, and for the past 20 minutes you have successfully resisted the impulse to open the lid and take a peek! Don't blow it now! LEAVE THE RICE ALONE!

6. While the rice continues cooking, sauté the bacon in a large frying pan. Reduce heat to medium low and let the fat render out of the bacon, about 10 minutes. Once the fat is released, remove the bacon, increase temperature to high, and add the peeled shrimp to the hot bacon fat. Season the shrimp lightly with salt, pepper, and a little cumin. Sauté the shrimp, flipping once after a minute or so, until they turn pink, about 3 minutes. DO NOT OVERCOOK! Remove shrimp from pan and set aside someplace where they will keep warm, but NOT continue cooking.

7. Okay, now you can check the rice. Open the lid and fluff the rice with a fork. Add the peas to the rice and carefully fold the cooked shrimp (throw in the bacon too, if you so desire, and we so desire to do this most of the time) into the rice and heat for about 3 additional minutes—just long enough to make sure everything is hot. Serve immediately.

THE CUBAN MELTING POT

MANY PEOPLE ARE surprised to learn that not all Cubans are descended from Spain, Africa, or the indigenous population of the island. There are French Cubans, Czech Cubans, Jewish Cubans, and somewhere there must be at least one Swedish Cuban! Another surprise is the number of Chinese Cubans. In fact, Havana was once home to Latin America's largest Chinatown! Chinese people first came to the island in the 1850s. Today there are tens of thousands of Cubans who have some Chinese heritage.

All Cuban families love to eat Chinese food on occasion, and many Chinese methods have melded with the Cuban ones. Arroz frito, or fried rice, has always been a favorite. When you eat so much rice, it's nice to try some new flavors now and then! The combinations are only limited by the imagination, and lechón asado con arroz frito *is not as far-fetched as it sounds.*

In America today, Latin fusion and Chino-Latino cuisine are all the rage. Well, we have some news for those big New York Nuevo-Latino chefs: "fusion" has been taking place in Cuba for decades. Either no one ever thought to call it that, or the people who started cooking food this way just didn't have a good publicist!

145

Jorge: Bacalao *is cod that has been salted and dried to preserve it.*

Glenn: *The best* bacalao *comes from Norway.*

Jorge: Bacalao *needs to be soaked in water overnight to remove the salt and reconstitute the fish.*

Glenn: *You might wonder, why not just use fresh cod? Well, the preserving process gives bacalao a distinctive flavor. Using real* bacalao *is essential in this recipe!*

Bacalao a la Cerito
Baked Codfish

· ·

INGREDIENTS

Serves 6 to 8

2	pounds bacalao (dried salted codfish)
5	cups thinly sliced Yukon Gold potatoes
	Salt for potatoes
2	large yellow onions, sliced thin in rings
5	cloves garlic, peeled and minced
1	green bell pepper, sliced in ¼-inch thick rings
¾	cup water
½	cup white wine
⅓	cup olive oil
¼	cup lime juice
1	(15-ounce) can tomato sauce
	Dash or two of Tabasco
1	small (4-ounce) jar capers, drained (optional)
1	red bell pepper, sliced in rings

146

1. Preheat oven to 375 degrees F.

2. Rinse the bacalao under cold running water for about 10 minutes. Cover the bacalao with water in a pan and soak overnight in the refrigerator. Drain. Cover with water, bring to a boil, reduce heat to low, cover, and cook until fish is soft. Drain water and crumble fish with a large fork.

TIP: Many people peel and quarter a raw potato and add it to the soaking bacalao. The potato draws off some of the salt from the water.

3. Lightly oil a flat casserole with a tablespoon of olive oil. Line the bottom with sliced potatoes. Salt the potatoes by eye with a shaker (pretend you are salting a fried egg and you will add just enough salt!). Cover the potatoes with bacalao, onion slices, minced garlic, and green pepper rings. Whisk together water, wine, oil, lime juice, tomato sauce, and Tabasco. Pour this mixture over the casserole. Sprinkle a handful of capers over the top if you like them.

4. Cover the pan with aluminum foil and bake in the oven, at 375 degrees F for approximately 25 to 40 minutes. It's done when the potatoes are cooked through. Garnish the top with red bell pepper slices.

Raúl: *We get this one all of the time: "Hey, Three Guys! I ordered the enchilada just like I always do at the local Taco Bell, but all I got was a bowl of fish stew."*

Glenn: *This is a common mistake in Cuban restaurants. An enchilado is a delicious stew made with fish and seafood.*

Jorge: *This one is best made with Florida lobsters, scallops, and shrimp. Or just use shrimp only to make enchilado de camarones (shrimp Creole).*

Enchilado de Mariscos
Seafood Creole

. . . .

INGREDIENTS

Serves 4 to 6

4	tablespoons butter
4	tablespoons olive oil
1	cup chopped green pepper
2½	cups chopped white onion
1	cup chopped celery
4	cloves garlic, minced
6	medium ripe Roma tomatoes, peeled and chopped
2	teaspoons ground cumin
¼	cup white wine
¼	cup water
¼	cup tomato juice
1	tablespoon lemon juice
½	teaspoon salt
¼	teaspoon freshly ground black pepper
2	Spanish chorizo links, casings removed, diced
	Olive oil for sautéing

1   pound shrimp, peeled, deveined, and butterflied

4   lobster tails, shell on, chopped in quarters

1   pound scallops

¼   cup chopped fresh cilantro

1. Melt the butter with the oil in a large pan on medium heat. Add the green pepper, onion, and celery, and sauté until the onion and celery are tender. Add the garlic and sauté an additional 1 or 2 minutes. Add the tomatoes, cumin, wine, water, tomato juice, lemon juice, salt, and pepper. Bring to a boil; reduce heat to low and simmer, uncovered, for about 15 minutes.

2. Meanwhile, remove the casings from the chorizo and sauté in a little olive oil until the oil turns orange. Remove the chorizo, keep the oil and sauté the seafood in small batches (don't crowd the pan) until the shrimp are bright, lobster tail chunks are bright pink and the scallops are firm and white.

3. Keep the seafood warm until you have finished sautéing all of it. Add the seafood to the pan of vegetables and sauce. Stir gently, adjusting seasonings as necessary. Simmer for 2 or 3 minutes only to meld the flavors, NO LONGER. You can add the cooked chorizo chunks to the dish, or just snack on them while you're cooking, as we always do! Remove from heat and sprinkle with fresh cilantro.

4. Serve over El Arroz Blanco Más Sabroso—The Ultimate White Rice (page 170).

Paella Cubana

Three Guys Cuban-Style Paella

• •

INGREDIENTS

Serves 8

½	cup olive oil (more or less)
1	cup diced ham
1	cup chorizo sausage, sliced into ½-inch pieces
2½	cups diced onion
1½	cups chopped green bell pepper
1½	cups chopped red bell pepper
6	cloves garlic, minced
4	cups chicken broth
¾	cup red wine
4	cans smoked clams or oysters with oil
	Dash of Bijol powder
8	bone-in, skin-on chicken thighs
3½	cups parboiled Valencia rice
2	teaspoons salt
4 to 8	medium lobster tails, meat removed from shell and cut in bite-size pieces

2 pounds medium raw shrimp, peeled and deveined

1½ pounds scallops

½ pound fresh or frozen crabmeat leg sections cut in pieces

Fresh clams or mussels in the shell (optional)

Water

Wine

1 cup frozen green peas

1 green or red bell pepper, sliced

1. Heat the olive oil in a LARGE pan. Sauté the ham and chorizo sausage. (Use only Spanish chorizo!) This will draw the oil from the chorizo and flavor the pan. Remove ham and chorizo and set aside.

2. Drop onion, green pepper, and red pepper in the remaining oil and cook until the onion is translucent. Add garlic and sauté briefly. In a large covered pot, add the broth, wine, smoked clams or oysters, onion-pepper mixture, and Bijol powder.

3. Fry chicken pieces in the remaining oil until browned on both sides. Remove chicken and set aside.

4. Add the chicken, ham, chorizo, rice, and salt to your pot. Bring to a boil, reduce heat to low, cover, and simmer on the stove for 30 to 40 minutes, until the rice is fully cooked. (The rice should be wet but not soupy at this point.)

5. While the rice is cooking, prepare the seafood for sautéing. It's important that the olive oil be "seasoned" with the chorizo, so sauté a few additional chorizo links as needed to give your oil a distinct pink appearance.

6. Carefully remove the lobster meat from the tails, keeping the shells whole so they can be used for a garnish. Cut up the lobster meat to give everyone a chance to taste this delicious treat!

7. When sautéing the seafood, undercook it just a bit. Shrimp and lobster will be pink; scallops will become white and less translucent. Crabmeat is usually

(continued on next page)

Raúl: *It's hard to complain about the food when your mouth is full of it!*

Glenn: *Many Latin paellas use beer. We like the mellower and less bitter flavor that a good, full-bodied red wine imparts to this dish.*

Jorge: *This is the dish we made for Tyler Florence when he came to Miami to tape an episode of "Tyler's Ultimate."*

Glenn: *We have made this recipe many times over the years and it has become our signature dish.*

Jorge: *We've done it so many times we could do it blindfolded!*

Paella Cubana (continuation)
Three Guys Cuban-Style Paella

. . . .

precooked, so a quick turn in the chorizo-flavored oil is all that's necessary to give it that extra flavor. Sauté the seafood in small batches. Don't overcrowd the pan! Remove each batch as you go and keep the seafood covered and warm so that it does not dry out.

8. If you have fresh clams and/or mussels, now is a good time to steam them in a little water and wine until they open. We like to use a New Zealand greenshell mussel, which comes precooked and frozen on the half shell. We simply steam them in a covered saucepan until just heated through.

9. Okay, the rice mixture is now completely cooked and all of the seafood has been sautéed. Gently fold the seafood into the rice mixture. Then spoon everything into a round flat pan suitable for serving. (We like to use a brown cazuela, a round terra-cotta dish that makes a nice presentation.) Garnish the top of the dish with crab leg sections, clams and mussels in the shell, frozen green peas, lobster tail shells, and green or red bell pepper.

10. Once you've assembled the paella in the cazuela, place the dish in a preheated 350-degree F. oven for 10 to 15 minutes, just long enough to meld the flavors and heat through. Do not overcook! Form a procession and carry the paella to the table with an elaborate flourish. Pause briefly at tableside to accept the voluminous applause of your dinner guests!

Glenn: *Red snapper is the most popular snapper in U.S. fish markets. You'll find this delicious fish all over the place.*

Jorge: *There are also other types of snapper that many remember eating in Cuba—the blue snapper, in particular.*

Raúl: *The mangrove snapper is abundant in Florida waters and very tasty!*

Glenn: *We usually cook this fish outside in a propane-fired deep fat fryer. It may also be prepared in an electric deep fryer or in a large frying pan on the stovetop. You need enough oil to completely immerse the whole fish.*

Jorge: *Deep-fat frying produces a very tender and juicy fish with a nice crispy crust. We give this dish a true island flavor with a delicious mango salsa. Be careful not to overcook your fish—it should be tender and flaky.*

Pargo Entero Frito con Salsa de Mango
Snapper with Mango Salsa

INGREDIENTS

Servings: Allow 1 medium-sized snapper per person. A very large fish can be served family style and sliced into serving portions at the table.

Several whole red, blue, or mangrove snappers, gutted and cleaned but with heads on

Juice of 1 lime

Garlic powder

Ground cumin

Salt and pepper

Salsa

1	cup chopped cilantro
½	cup finely chopped green onion
½	cup finely chopped green pepper
1	cup mashed fresh ripe mango
	Juice of 1 lime
⅛	teaspoon salt to taste
	Red pepper flakes
¼	cup cubed mango

Oil for deep-fat frying

Flour for dusting

154

1. Depending on the size of the fish, make 1 to 3 deep diagonal slashes on one side of the fish with a sharp knife.

2. Lightly sprinkle both sides of each fish with the lime juice. Season lightly with garlic powder, cumin, salt, and pepper. Let fish rest for 20 minutes in the refrigerator. Soft music and subdued lighting will enhance the resting process.

3. While the fish are enjoying their well-deserved rest, make the salsa by mixing the cilantro, green onion, green pepper, mashed mango, and lime juice in a small bowl. Add a little salt at a time and taste—adjust the amount of salt to taste. Add a pinch of red pepper flakes for a little bite. Finally, add some cubed mango pieces for a nice presentation.

4. Heat the oil to the proper temperature for deep-fat frying—about 375 degrees F. Just before dropping into the oil, lightly dust fish on both sides with a little white flour. Cook two or three fish at a time in the hot oil until cooked through. The fish cooks fast, approximately 3 to 5 minutes, depending on the size of the fish, so don't let it get away from you!

SALSA DE MANGO
Add a little Mango Salsa (page 154) to any dish for a refreshingly fruity taste!

A CUBAN FISH STORY

On an island surrounded by water you'd think the people of Cuba would be eating fresh fish every day. Even in pre-Castro times, it was rare to see fresh fish very far inland from the coast. Cuba just didn't have the infrastructure—refrigerated warehouses, trucks, retail stores—to keep the fish fresh from boat to market. By the 1960s, most seafood caught by Cuban fisheries was dedicated to the export market. The only fish the Castillos and Musibays saw was a rare shipment of mackerel caught by the fishing fleet in Peru and frozen in huge solid blocks. These blocks could be shipped inland from the coast with some success. Even in the tropical heat, a large block of ice takes awhile to completely melt. However, if you had to rely on the government stores for fish, you were lucky to get some once a month. In really bad times, the fish was available only in pre-ground breaded patties.

Raúl has always been an avid sports fisherman, and when he lived in Cuba he frequently brought home crappies and trout from one of Cuba's freshwater lakes or lagoons. Raúl and Jorge also occasionally got to do some ocean fishing, mostly for red and blue snapper. Many Cubans fish from shore using kites to carry their bait far enough away from the shore. Another popular method is to fish from a large inner tube from a truck tire. This is so popular that the people who do this even have a nickname: *neumáticos.*

Glenn: *Cubans frequently use marinades to infuse meat or fish with delicious spices. This recipe gives fish a wonderful citrus flavor without being too heavy.*

Raúl: *This recipe works great with just about any type of fish fillet. For me, it is usually whatever fish I caught the day before! Make sure to leave the skin on.*

Jorge: *The skin will keep the fillets from shrinking and will keep the fish from sticking to the grill.*

Glenn: *Once the fish is done, you can easily remove the skin before serving. Or leave it on if you like!*

Pescado de Habana
Grilled Fish Havana-Style

. . . .

INGREDIENTS

Allow approximately ¾ pound of fish per person.

¼	cup olive oil
6	garlic cloves
1	cup onion
1	teaspoon ground cumin
2	teaspoons oregano
1	teaspoon salt
¼	cup fresh cilantro
	Juice of one lime
2	tablespoons vinegar
¼	cup white wine
2	to 3 pounds (approximately) fish fillets (grouper, salmon, kingfish, tuna), skin on
	Salt and pepper to taste

1. Run all ingredients (except the fish fillets, obviously—wow, what a mess that would make!) through the blender until the onions are finely chopped. Place fillets in a shallow dish and pour marinade on top. Cover and marinate 2 to 4 hours in the refrigerator—no longer! Otherwise you'll have pickled fish!

2. Make sure your grill is well oiled, the coals are hot and ready, or the gas grill is fully flamed and sizzling. Just before cooking, remove the fillets from the marinade and pat dry with a paper towel. Rub a little olive oil on the flesh side of the fish and place the fillets on the grill skin side up just long enough to put some nice grill marks on the flesh. Then carefully use a steel spatula to flip the fillets skin side down.

3. Flip the fillets once and once only! Cover your grill and continue cooking until fish flakes with a fork. Keep an eye out for any flare-ups so the fish doesn't burn. Salt and pepper to taste before serving.

Picadillo de Pescado

Cuban Fish Hash

. . . .

INGREDIENTS

Serves 6

2	pounds red snapper fillets, skinned and deboned
	Salt and pepper to taste
½	cup white wine
½	cup water
2	cups chopped onion
2	cups chopped green pepper
	Olive oil for sautéing
4	cloves garlic
1	cup diced red Roma tomatoes
6	slices day-old Cuban or French bread
½	cup milk (approximately)
2	teaspoons ground cumin
	Juice of 1 lime
	Salt and pepper to taste

Jorge: *This is a special* picadillo. *Instead of ground beef, it uses fish.*

Raúl: *We like to serve this when we have people over, especially nice for a Sunday brunch!*

Glenn: *For many Cuban Catholics, this is also a great way to enjoy* picadillo *on Fridays during Lent.*

158

1. Season the fish with salt and pepper and place in a covered sauté pan. Cover and poach the fish in the wine and water until the fish is flaky, turning once. (The exact cooking time depends on the thickness of your fish. Check after 5 minutes.) Pour off the liquids and break the fish into chunks with a fork. Cover and set fish aside in a warm place.

2. Sauté the onion and green pepper in olive oil until they start to get limp. Add the garlic and tomatoes and continue sautéing for an additional 1 or 2 minutes.

3. Place the bread in a mixing bowl and soak with milk. Break up the bread with your fingers and add to the pan, stirring until thoroughly mixed.

4. Gently fold in the cooked fish. Add the cumin and lime juice. Salt and pepper to taste. Cook just long enough to meld the flavors together and heat through.

5. Serve over El Arroz Blanco Más Sabroso—The Ultimate White Rice (page 170).

Jorge: *We never had any salmon in Cuba!*

Raúl: *But many Cuban exiles have learned to love this cold-water fish.*

Glenn: *They sell a lot of salmon in the Miami area. When the price is good, Raúl loves to buy about 10 pounds and have a huge cookout.*

Raúl: *This recipe is simple and easy to prepare. You can hardly go wrong with this one!*

Salmón de Raúl a la Parilla

Raúl's Salmon Grilled in Foil

. . . .

INGREDIENTS

Serves 4

- 2 pounds salmon fillets (not steaks)
  Olive oil
  Sazón Goya or Sazón Tropical (lightly sprinkled)
- 1 cup sliced onion
- 3 large celery stalks, sliced into 3 x ¾-inch strips
  Fresh lime juice

- ½ cup real mayonnaise
- 2 tablespoons fresh lime juice
  Tabasco

1. Carefully remove the skin from the salmon fillet with a sharp thin knife. Cut the salmon lengthwise down the middle to separate the thicker upper body section from the thinner underbelly. Cut the salmon into serving-size pieces, about 4 inches wide.

2. Lightly rub the salmon fillet with olive oil and place on a sheet of aluminum foil. Sprinkle the fish with Sazón Goya. Place onion and celery on top of the fish. Add a dash of lime juice and another dash of Sazón Goya. (NOTE: If you can't find Sazón Goya or Sazón Tropical locally, please consult Sources on page 224.)

3. Fold the sheet of aluminum foil over to make a pouch, crimping all edges. Place fish on a hot grill. Put the thicker pieces on the grill first—they'll take 15 to 20 minutes to cook. Add the thinner pieces about 8 to 10 minutes after the thicker ones. That way all of the fish will be cooked completely (but not overcooked) at the same time. Remove the individual servings from the foil.

TIP: If you want to add a smoky flavor, add some wood chips to your grill fire and open the foil on each packet for the last 1 or 2 minutes.

4. While the fish is cooking, mix mayonnaise with lime juice and a 1 or 2 (or 3 or more!) drops of Tabasco. Taste the mayonnaise and add more lime as desired. Just before serving, place a generous dollop of the mayonnaise mixture on each fillet. Garnish with the cooked onion and celery from the packet. Serve hot.

PAPAS APLASTADAS
If you're looking for a dish full of flavor, try some Cuban Crushed Potatoes (recipe page 186).

Side Dishes

Glenn: *This has to be one of our most requested recipes. It's also a recipe I like to make at home. The kids love it and it's a great dish to prepare for guests.*

Jorge: *And it's not that hard to make!*

Glenn: *Don't let the rather long list of ingredients scare you! You can do everything in this recipe with less than an hour's prep time.*

Raúl: *And that includes drinking a beer or two!*

Arroz Imperial
Imperial Rice

. . . .

INGREDIENTS

Serves 8 to 10

CHICKEN MIXTURE:

3	pounds chicken thighs, skin on
8	cups water
	Olive oil
4	strips bacon, cut into slivers
1½	cups finely chopped white onion
2	cups cored, seeded, and chopped green pepper
3	green onions, trimmed and chopped
1	teaspoon oregano
5	large cloves garlic, minced
1	(15-ounce) can tomato sauce
1	tablespoon dry sherry
½	cup frozen green peas
	Juice of 1 medium lime
	Salt and pepper to taste

1. Wash chicken and place in an 8-quart stockpot. Add approximately 8 cups of water to fully cover meat. Bring to a boil, reduce heat to low, and simmer, uncovered, until the meat is tender and falls from the bone— approximately 45 minutes to 1 hour. Remove chicken and reserve the broth. (You will use some of the broth to make the rice.) Skim excess fat

from broth. When completely cooled, skin and break the chicken into small pieces by hand. (Feed chicken skin to dog or other suitable receptacle.)

2. Sauté the bacon briefly in a large sauté pan. Drain most, but not all, of the excess fat. You can blot it up with a paper towel (be careful not to let the hot grease touch your fingers). Add a tiny bit of olive oil and heat. Add onion, green pepper, green onion, and oregano. Sauté until the onion is translucent. Add the garlic and sauté for an additional minute, stirring occasionally. Add tomato sauce, chicken, and sherry. Bring to a boil, reduce heat to low, and simmer, uncovered, approximately 15 minutes to thicken the sauce. Add peas and lime juice during the last 5 minutes of cooking. Salt and pepper to taste. TASTE IT! Set aside.

3. Preheat oven to 325 degrees F.

To Cook Rice:

7	cups chicken broth (from the cooked chicken above)
4	cups parboiled rice
1	teaspoon salt
2	teaspoons Bijol powder

To Assemble Dish:

7	tablespoons real mayonnaise
⅔	cup (approximately) grated Parmesan cheese (for a sharper taste, use half Parmesan, half Romano)
½	pound Monterey Jack or other mild white cheese, grated

1. Mix the rice with the chicken broth in a covered 3-quart saucepan; add salt and Bijol powder for color—if you can't get this locally, use a little yellow food coloring. Bring to a boil, reduce heat to low, cover, and cook until the rice is thoroughly cooked and most of the broth has been absorbed.

2. Add the mayonnaise a little at a time to the cooked rice, mixing thoroughly. Take a third of the rice and cover the bottom of a 9 x 13-inch pan. Layer chicken mixture on top of the rice, then add a layer of the mayonnaise/rice mixture.

(continued on next page)

165

Arroz Imperial (continuation)
Imperial Rice

3. Generously sprinkle Parmesan cheese on top of this layer. Add the remaining rice. Again, sprinkle Parmesan cheese on the top layer. Spread grated Monterey Jack or another mild white cheese completely over the top.

4. Bake for about 15 to 20 minutes, or until the cheese melts completely and bubbles, browning slightly.

Calabaza a la Parilla

Calabaza on the Grill

. . . .

INGREDIENTS

Serves 4

1	large calabaza
⅓	cup Spanish olive oil
3	tablespoons fresh lime juice
	Salt and pepper to taste

1. Cut the calabaza in half and remove all the seeds and fibers. Slice the calabaza as you would a cantaloupe and remove the rind.

2. Whisk the olive oil with the lime juice. Drizzle this oil mixture over the calabaza slices. Salt and pepper to taste. Grill calabaza outdoors on the barbecue, brushing occasionally with the oil.

3. Slices are done when they are tender and lightly browned. Serve as a side dish with your favorite grilled meat.

Glenn: *Calabaza is the great pumpkin! Not the one in the comic strip, but a type of cooking pumpkin used in Cuban cuisine.*

Jorge: *When a Cuban recipe calls for pumpkin, don't even think of substituting one of those big orange Halloween varieties!*

Raúl: *The calabaza is more closely related to squash, with a firm flesh and mild flavor.*

Jorge: *A nice way to develop a taste for this Cuban treat is to prepare some on the grill. If you're in an area where you just can't get real calabaza, you might try butternut squash. The flavor and texture are similar, although not exactly the same.*

167

Jorge: *The sauce is called "chimichurri" and is used on many types of Cuban- and Argentine-style steaks. Our Nicaraguan in-laws love it.*

Raúl: *We've also seen it served at the table for dipping in many restaurants, with a fresh loaf of Cuban bread. Delicious!*

Glenn: *I'll never forget the time I brought some Chimichurri to a Minnesota barbeque. When I put the Chimichurri on my steak hot off the grill, I got a lot of weird stares and comments. "Wow, what's that green stuff?" I persuaded a few people to try a little with their steaks and, as they say, the rest is history.*

Raúl: *It happens all the time. Some people have convinced themselves that they're not going to like a certain type of food. Once they try it— wow—they love it!*

Glenn: *The typical Argentine version of Chimichurri is made with parsley. In our "Cubanized" version, we use cilantro instead—it gives it a great flavor, much more intense than the regular variety.*

168

Chimichurri
Sauce for Meat

. . . .

INGREDIENTS

1	cup cilantro leaves
8	cloves garlic
¼	cup vinegar
	Juice of one lime
½	cup onion
	Dash or two of red pepper flakes
⅔	cup olive oil
	Salt and pepper to taste
½	cup chopped sweet red peppers (optional)
½	cup minced tomato (optional)
½	cup chopped fresh oregano (optional)

1. Put the cilantro, garlic, vinegar, lime juice, onion, and red pepper flakes in a blender; using the "chop" setting, click on and off until the mixture is thick. Do not overprocess!

2. Pour the mixture into a large, non-metallic bowl. Whisk in the olive oil by hand. If you use the blender to incorporate the oil, the liquids will emulsify, giving your chimichurri a white, unappetizing, paste-like texture.

3. Add salt and pepper, plus more vinegar and lime juice as needed. The flavor should be very intense with garlic and cilantro. Don't be stingy with the salt either!

4. This is the kind of dish you need to taste and adjust so that you get just the right flavor. The best way to taste it is with a piece of bread. We have sometimes gone through a whole loaf of bread this way. So, please, be responsible and limit your tasting to a slice of bread or two! Or, better yet, double the recipe and have plenty of chimichurri for both eating and snacking!

5. Several restaurants vary the dish by including some or all of the optional additions. However, it tastes just fine without them. See what you like—experiment! (If you do want to experiment, just fold in the optional ingredients.)

El Arroz Blanco Más Sabroso

The Ultimate White Rice

. . . .

INGREDIENTS

Serves 4 "regular" people or 2 hungry Cubans

NOTE: To serve 8 "regular" people or 4 hungry Cubans, double all ingredients. To serve 12 "regular" people or 8 hungry Cubans, triple all ingredients. To serve 16 "regular" people or—well, you get the idea.

- 2 cups parboiled white rice
- 3 cups water
- 1 teaspoon salt
- 1 clove garlic, peeled
- 1 tablespoon olive oil

1. Place the rice in a strainer or colander and run under cold water for a couple of minutes to rinse thoroughly. Use one of the following methods for cooking the rice:

A. If you have a rice cooker, place the rice in the rice cooker's pot. Add water, salt, garlic, and olive oil; stir. Turn or click the switch to the "cook" position. When the rice is done, the rice cooker will revert to a warming mode automatically. Fluff cooked rice with a fork and serve hot. Always follow your rice cooker manufacturer's instructions, as different brands and models may vary.

B. If you don't have a rice cooker, place the rice in a large covered saucepan. Add water, salt, garlic, and olive oil; stir. Bring to a boil over high heat and cook, uncovered, for 2 or 3 minutes, or until the surface of your rice looks like the surface of the moon—full of craters! Immediately cover, reduce heat to low, and simmer for about 15 to 20 minutes. Fluff cooked rice with a fork and serve hot.

Glenn: *If there is such a thing as a Cuban signature dish, it would have to be* frijoles negros.

Jorge: *In Cuba, you'd* NEVER *see a meal served without black beans and rice! In Miami and other exile communities, the tradition continues.*

Glenn: *The original Indian population of Cuba ate black beans long before the Europeans arrived. Eating black beans traces its roots to the very beginnings of Cuban civilization.*

Raúl: *Black beans have as many cooking methods as there are "civilized" Cuban cooks!*

Jorge: *Every Cuban chef has a special ingredient or two to throw into the mix. Great* frijoles negros *should be soft and a little mushy—the beans break open when they cook and make a rich black broth.*

Glenn: *Black beans can also be a complete meal with the addition of meat—with ham, with bits of* chicharrones, *or even with leftover* lechón *cooked into the mix. Very tasty!*

172

Frijoles Negros
Black Beans
. . . .

INGREDIENTS

Serves 8

2½	cups dried black beans
8	cups water
1	tablespoon olive oil
1½	cups chopped onion
1½	cups chopped green pepper
3	cloves garlic mashed with 1 teaspoon salt and ½ teaspoon black peppercorns
	Olive oil for sautéing
1	teaspoon oregano
1	teaspoon ground cumin
1	bay leaf
3	tablespoons vinegar
6	ounces dry Spanish wine
	Salt and pepper to taste
2	teaspoons sugar
	Olive oil
	Cilantro (optional)
	White onion, chopped (optional)

1. Place the cleaned black beans in a 6-quart saucepan. Add water and olive oil—this will prevent the beans from foaming. Bring the beans to a boil, reduce heat to low, cover, and cook until the beans are tender—about 1 hour. DO NOT ADD SALT to the beans when they are cooking! Salt at this stage of the game will make your beans very tough!

2. You may, instead, cook the beans in a pressure cooker. Follow the manufacturer's directions for exact times, but our pressure cooker takes about 20 to 25 minutes to cook the beans completely.

3. Whichever method you use, DO NOT DRAIN the water from the cooked beans!

4. Meanwhile, chop onion and green pepper. Mash the garlic with salt and peppercorns with a mortar and pestle. Sauté onion and green pepper in olive oil until onion is translucent. Add mashed garlic and sauté another minute or so.

5. Add the cooked beans, oregano, cumin, bay leaf, vinegar, and wine. Cover and simmer on low heat for 15 to 20 minutes, stirring occasionally. Remove bay leaf.

6. Some cooks like to thicken the beans by taking about 1 cup of beans and mashing them slightly to make a thick paste. Mix mashed beans back into the pot.

7. Add more salt and pepper to taste. Stir in the sugar; then drizzle several tablespoons of olive oil over the beans. Immediately cover the pot and remove from heat; let stand for 10 minutes.

8. Serve these fantastically prepared black beans (aren't you proud of yourself?) over white rice. You may garnish the beans with cilantro and chopped white onions. Not only do they look good presented this way, but they taste even better than they look!

BLACK BEANS
(Frijoles Negros)

*I*N A CUBAN *household, black beans are eaten with just about every meal. Traditionalists would* NEVER *use canned black beans in any recipe. Black beans from a can? Horrors! Making black beans from scratch is not difficult; it just takes a little bit longer.*

IMPORTANT: *No matter what the brand or how much you pay for them, just about every bag of dried black beans has at least one thing in the bag that you* DON'T *want to serve on your plate. Usually it's a small stone, a piece of grit, or just a bad bean. So when preparing dried black beans, it's vital to carefully pick through the beans and remove the occasional stowaway. Discard any broken bean or any bean that floats to the top when you pour into the water. No, you didn't buy a bad bag of beans—it's just a natural part of the mysterious bean harvesting process.*

Over the past twenty years, black beans have become very popular in the United States. You can find dried black beans at your corner supermarket just about anywhere—even in Dubuque! We'll also let you in on a little secret: there probably isn't a Cuban cook out there who hasn't had to resort to a can or two of black beans to speed things up in a pinch. Well, except for Jorge's mother!

Jorge: Fufú *is a delicious dish, similar to mashed potatoes.*

Glenn: Fufú *has a delicious garlic flavor with a hint of lemon or lime.*

Jorge: *What really makes it sing are the delicious pieces of roast pork that are mashed into the plantain.*

Raúl: *You'll never find fufú on the menu at your local McDonald's!*

Fufú

Mashed Plantains

. . . .

INGREDIENTS

Serves 4

3	large plantains
4	cups chicken stock
½	pound pork meat with fat
	Water
3	cloves garlic, mashed
⅓	cup chopped green onions
4	tablespoons soft butter
	Salt and pepper to taste
	Fresh lemon juice

1. Cut the ends off the plantains and discard. Slice each plantain into 2-inch chunks and score the skin with a knife along one edge. DO NOT PEEL. Place the plantains in a 3-quart saucepan, and add the chicken stock. Bring to a boil, reduce heat to low, cover, and simmer until tender.

2. For meat, you need pork with plenty of fat—either well marbled or with a fat layer or both. We've had good luck with deboned pork ribs. Or have the butcher cut something to order.

3. Whichever meat you use, you need to slice it into small pieces—approximately 2 inches square. Salt by eye with a shaker and place in a 3-quart saucepan. Add water to just barely cover. Bring to a boil, reduce heat to low, and simmer, uncovered, until all of the water has boiled away. Do we really need to tell you to keep an eye on it? Good, we didn't think so! There should be a small quantity of rendered liquid fat in the bottom of the pan. You may need to add a little olive oil if your pork is a little on the lean side.

4. Fry the pork pieces in the rendered fat just until brown but NOT crispy! The meat should be tender and stringy. Remove the meat. Use a meat hammer to mash and otherwise pulverize the meat into small shreds.

5. Sauté the garlic and onion in the rendered fat at medium temperature for 3 to 5 minutes. Return meat to the pan.

6. Remove the fully cooked plantains from the broth (save the broth) and remove the peels (they should be falling off by now).

7. Mash the plantains with a hand masher and a little of the broth, just enough to make a soft, thick paste—like mashed potatoes. Don't be afraid if you have lumps of plantain—that's actually a good thing in this dish. Mash in the softened butter. Add the mashed plantain to the fried pork and onions, stirring constantly over low heat. Salt and pepper to taste. Give the whole works a generous squirt of lemon juice. Serve hot.

TIP: Some cooks use green plantains and some use very ripe plantains for this dish. We like to use plantains with a few flecks of black spotting—they have just a touch of sweetness.

Glenn: *On our first trip to California we noticed that just about every Cuban restaurant provided extra mojo sauce for adding to the main dish, something we don't see that much in Miami.*

Jorge: *They run their mojo through a blender, which emulsifies the oil and the liquid, giving the mojo a thick white look.*

Glenn: *It looks a bit like creamy Italian dressing, but it tastes like good mojo with a crisp garlic and citrus flavor. It's usually served on the side in a little serving dish about the size of a shot glass.*

Jorge: *If you're like Raúl, you may be tempted to finish your meal by taking any leftover garlic sauce and tossing it back like a shot of tequila.*

Raúl: *You've never heard of an after-dinner drink?*

L.A. Garlic Sauce

. . . .

INGREDIENTS

5	cloves of garlic
½	cup olive oil
2	tablespoons white vinegar
½	cup sour orange juice (see page 109)
	Salt and pepper to taste

1. Place the garlic, olive oil, and white vinegar in a food processor and puree until you have a smooth, white paste. Continue blending and gradually add the sour orange juice. Salt and pepper to taste.

2. Use as a dip, on bread, with chicken, on a hot dog, with your favorite breakfast cereal—the possibilities are limited only by your imagination!

WHERE ARE THE VEGETABLES?

*O*NE THING PEOPLE *quickly notice about Cuban cuisine—there aren't a lot of vegetable dishes. In a land where just about anything grows under the tropical sun and abundant rain, you'd think a wide selection of vegetables would be natural. However, Cubans are not known for eating a lot of green vegetables. In Cuban cuisine, most of the vegetables eaten are starchy root vegetables, beans, and of course, plantains.*

One green vegetable that Cubans love is tomatoes. The tomatoes are picked while they are still green and typically served thinly sliced with a dash of olive oil, a dash of lime juice, salt, and pepper. If you grow tomatoes in your home garden, pick a few while they are still green and try serving them in this very typical Cuban fashion!

177

Jorge: *There are many variations of mojo. It is the signature marinade of Cuba and it finds its way into many different dishes. Some mojos include oil. However, when you are roasting pork or a whole pig, the oil is not necessary—there's plenty of fat in the pig.*

Glenn: *The key element is sour orange, an almost bitter orange that grows throughout Cuba. Many Cubans brought the sour orange to South Florida, where it also flourishes.*

Raúl: *But it's hard to find in many parts of the country. You can buy some at many Latin groceries or online in bottles.*

Jorge: *Or just use our handy "sour orange juice substitute" recipe on page 109.*

Mojo
Cuban Marinade

. . . .

INGREDIENTS

8	to 10 cloves garlic
1	teaspoon salt
½	teaspoon black peppercorns (whole)
1	teaspoon oregano
¾	cup sour orange juice (see page 109)

1. The key to making mojo is in the proportions. Keep all the dry ingredients in approximately the proportions of the basic recipe above and you can't go wrong! And the nice thing is, you can make exactly the amount you need.

2. For a whole pig, we use four or five large HEADS of garlic (70 to 80 cloves) and approximately 1 quart of sour orange juice. For a large Lechón Asado (page 120), we use about 15 to 20 cloves of garlic and approximately 2 cups of sour orange juice. For Masitas de Puerco Fritas (page 122), we use about 8 to 12 cloves of garlic and approximately 1 cup of sour orange juice.

3. Use a mortar and pestle. Add approximately 10 cloves of garlic, ½ teaspoon salt, some black peppercorns, and some oregano. Mash them all together into a paste. Scoop the paste out into a separate bowl. Continue this process until all of the garlic is mashed.

4. Stir in ¾ cup sour orange juice. Let sit at room temperature for 30 minutes or longer. Use immediately to season the pig, or refrigerate for later use.

TIP: If you are making your own sour orange juice and it doesn't taste very tart, add a little white vinegar.

Jorge: *The dark-skinned Moors invaded Spain in the eighth century, making a lasting impact on Spanish culture. In this dish, the beans represent the Moors and the white rice represents the Spaniards.*

Glenn: *Frijoles Negro— Black Beans is traditionally served with the prepared beans on top of cooked, white rice.*

Raúl: *Unlike Moros y Cristianos, where the rice and beans are cooked together in a perfect example of Cuban unity.*

Moros y Cristianos
Moors and Christians

. . . .

INGREDIENTS

Serves 8

1½	cups dry black beans
4	cups water
3	cups long-grain white rice
2½	cups diced white onion
2½	cups seeded and chopped green peppers
¼	cup olive oil for sautéing
4	cloves garlic, crushed and chopped
2	tablespoons tomato paste
2	teaspoons ground cumin
1	teaspoon oregano
1	bay leaf
3	tablespoons white vinegar
4½	cups chicken stock
2	teaspoons salt
½	teaspoon pepper
	Olive oil (optional)
	Parsley or cilantro for garnish (optional)

1. Cover the dry beans with about 4 cups water in a 3-quart saucepan. DON'T add any salt yet! Bring to a boil, and boil for 3 minutes. Remove from the heat and let stand, covered, for 1 hour. Drain and rinse the beans. Add enough water to cover once again and bring to a boil; reduce heat to low, cover, and cook until tender—about 40 to 50 minutes. Drain.

2. Rinse the rice with cold water until the water runs clear.

3. Use an 8-quart covered stockpot with lid. Sauté the onion and green pepper in the olive oil until tender. Add the garlic and sauté another minute or so. Add the tomato paste, black beans, cumin, oregano, bay leaf, and vinegar. Cook for about 5 minutes, stirring gently.

4. Add the chicken stock and the rinsed rice. Bring to a boil, reduce heat to low, cover, and simmer for about 20 to 30 minutes, or until rice is fully cooked.

5. Finally, adjust the seasonings by adding salt and pepper to taste. Remove the bay leaf. Serve hot.

6. For an added treat, drizzle a little olive oil over the rice in the pot and fluff cooked rice gently with a fork. If plating the rice as a side dish, drizzle a little olive oil over individual servings and garnish with some parsley or cilantro.

Glenn: *Although there are some limited areas of the country where you can get a decent loaf of Cuban bread (cities like Los Angeles and Union City, New Jersey), the best Cuban bread is made in south Florida. In fact, the "Cuban Bread Line" (the Mason-Dixon line of Cuban pastry) stretches across the state just north of Tampa. Stray north of the Cuban Bread Line and you have two chances of getting a decent loaf: slim and none.*

Jorge: *Yes, you can find Cuban bread at practically every supermarket in Miami. However, the big chain groceries have never quite gotten it right.*

Glenn: *Although these store-made loaves will do in a pinch, the only place to get the real thing is from a Cuban bread bakery. And if you don't have a Cuban bakery in your town, you have to make it yourself!*

Jorge: *This recipe is the real deal. You CANNOT make Cuban bread without lard. If it doesn't have lard, it's NOT Cuban bread, so please don't substitute!*

Pan Cubano

Cuban Bread

. . . .

INGREDIENTS

Makes one large wide loaf

1	tablespoon active dry yeast
2	teaspoons sugar
1¼	cups warm water
2	teaspoons salt
2	cups bread flour (see instructions)
2	cups all purpose flour (see instructions)
¼	cup lard, melted in microwave
	Warm water, to brush on loaves before baking

1. Grease a large bowl and set aside.

2. Take a small bowl and dissolve the yeast and sugar in ¼ cup of warm (110 degrees F) water. Place the bowl in a warm place and let it stand until it starts to foam and doubles in volume, about 10 minutes. If it doesn't foam and bubble, you have some bad yeast!

3. Meanwhile, measure out ¼ cup of lard and place the lard in a Pyrex measuring cup or other suitable container. Heat in the microwave on high for about 90 seconds, or until melted.

4. Place the water/yeast/sugar mixture in the mixing bowl of a stand mixer. Add the rest of the warm water and the salt. Using the dough hook, mix on low speed until blended.

5. Take your measuring cup and dig into the flour bag, scooping out 2 whole cups of each flour. Now the important part: in a separate bowl, sift together the two flours. Sifted flour has more volume than unsifted flour, so you will use approximately 3¼ cups of sifted flour in the following steps.

6. Gradually add the flour mixture, a little at a time, to the wet ingredients in your mixer, mixing constantly. At the same time you are adding flour, gradually pour in the melted lard. Keep adding a little flour and a little lard until all of the lard has been added.

7. Continue adding more flour—A LITTLE AT A TIME—until you make a smooth and pliable dough. Try to add just enough flour to make the dough elastic—just as much as necessary for the dough hook to barely clean the sides of the bowl. Too much flour and your bread will be too dense! You will use approximately 3¼ cups of sifted flour to bring the dough to this point. (More or less; this is where the art of baking comes in.) Save any leftover flour mixture for rolling out the dough.

8. Now let the machine and the dough hook go to work kneading the dough. Set the mixer on a low speed and knead for about 3 to 4 minutes—no more! Your dough will be fairly sticky at this point.

NOTE: If you don't have a mixer with a dough hook, you can also do this the old-fashioned way. Turn the dough out onto a lightly floured surface. Pound the dough ball down and knead by hand until the dough is smooth and elastic, about 10 minutes.

(continued on next page)

BAKING BREAD IS AN ART

Baking bread, any kind of bread, is truly an art. Baking a perfect bakery-quality loaf of Cuban bread is the ultimate accomplishment for any home bread baker. On the surface, Cuban bread seems so simple; it consists of just five main ingredients: flour, water, yeast, lard, and salt. The challenge, however, is putting these simple ingredients together in exactly the right way. The goal is to create a loaf with a crisp crust on the outside and an airy, lightly textured inside.

The key to baking a great loaf of Cuban bread is in knowing exactly how much flour to use to bring the dough to the perfect consistency. Too much flour, and the bread will be too dense. Too little flour, and the dough won't rise properly, resulting in a very wide, flat loaf of bread. If you don't mind a challenge, the quest for that perfect loaf of Cuban bread can be very rewarding. A warm, fresh-baked loaf of Cuban bread is the next best thing to heaven!

Pan Cubano (continuation)
Cuban Bread

. . . .

9. Shape the dough into a ball (yes, it's a little sticky, but you can do it!) and place it into the bowl you originally greased in the first step of this recipe—what was that, something like a week ago now? We know, we know—bread making is a long and involved process!

10. Flip the dough ball a few times to grease it up on all sides. Cover the bowl with a damp cloth and put in a warm place. (We like to preheat our oven to 160 degrees F and then turn it off, thus creating a perfectly warm environment for our rising bread.) Let the dough rise until it doubles in size—about 45 minutes to 1 hour. It's at this point in the process that you can usually find three guys, covered in flour, sitting by the pool with their feet up and enjoying a cold beverage. It's also about now when Raúl always asks, "Why didn't we just pick up a loaf of bread at the bakery?"

11. When you return from the pool, turn the dough out onto a lightly floured board, using the leftover flour you have in the bowl. Sprinkle some flour on the dough and use a rolling pin to roll it out. We like to make a large loaf, shaped to fit our longest baking sheet diagonally—about 20 inches long. So we try to roll out a 12 x 20-inch rectangle. Sprinkle more flour on the dough and turn it over a few times as you roll it out, to keep it from sticking to the rolling pin. The added flour at this rolling stage should take care of most of the stickiness of the dough.

12. Roll the dough up into a tightly rolled long cylinder, with a slight taper at both ends. Wet your fingers and pinch the loose flap of the rolled dough into the loaf, making a tight seam.

13. Grease a baking sheet and sprinkle lightly with cornmeal.

14. Place the loaf diagonally onto the baking sheet, seam side down. Dust the top with a little extra flour and cover very loosely with plastic wrap. (You don't want the rising dough to dry out or stick to the plastic wrap.) Place in a warm spot and allow the loaf to stand and rise once again until it is about 2½ times it's original size—about 45 minutes to 1 hour. Cuban bread is wider than French bread, so expect your loaf to spread out quite a bit as it rises.

15. Preheat oven to 450 degrees F. Place a pan of water on the lowest rack of the oven.

16. Use a sharp knife to cut a shallow seam down the middle of the top of the bread, leaving about two inches of uncut top on each end of the loaf.

17. Brush the top of the loaf with water and place in your preheated oven on the middle shelf. After about 5 minutes of baking, brush some more water on top of the bread. Bake the loaf until it is light brown and crusty—about 12 to 18 minutes total baking time.

18. We all know that oven temperatures vary, so keep an eye on it!

Glenn: *Cubans are known for eating many types of root vegetables: yuca, malanga, boniato.*

Jorge: *But we do also enjoy potatoes, the number one root vegetable of Americans!*

Raúl: *This recipe uses new potatoes, the small red ones you see in the supermarket.*

Glenn: *The skin of the new potato is very thin, so leave it on! It gives this dish a great flavor and nice color.*

Papas Aplastadas
Crushed Potatoes

. . . .

INGREDIENTS

Serves 4

4	strips of bacon, chopped
12 to 16	new potatoes, unpeeled (golf-ball size)
1	cup chopped green pepper
	Olive oil
3	cloves garlic, minced
	Salt to taste
½	teaspoon black pepper to taste
1½	teaspoons cumin to taste
¾	cup chopped green onion
½	cup grated sharp cheddar cheese
½	cup grated Monterrey Jack cheese

1. Cover potatoes with lightly salted water. Bring to a boil, reduce heat to low, cover, and simmer for about 15 to 20 minutes, or until the potatoes are fork-tender. Remove from heat and drain.

2. While the potatoes are cooking, sauté chopped bacon in a large frying pan until crispy. Remove bacon bits but do not drain the oil.

3. Add the green pepper and a little olive oil to the pan and sauté until tender. Add the minced garlic and sauté an additional minute or so only.

4. Lightly grease a jelly roll pan, pizza pan, or baking sheet; you need a flat pan with a raised edge that can go under the broiler. Arrange the cooked potatoes on the pan. Spray the bottom of a coffee cup with some vegetable spray, and use the cup to smash the potatoes until they are crushed and flattened in a thin layer that more or less covers the bottom of the pan. Crush—don't mash—the potatoes! They should look like you dropped them on the floor, NOT like you ran over them with your SUV!

5. Drizzle the potatoes liberally with olive oil and sprinkle to taste with salt, pepper, and cumin. The amounts listed in the ingredients are approximate. The best way is to start conservatively, taste a bite of the potato, and add more spices as needed! Top the potatoes with the green pepper, green onion, and bacon bits.

6. Spread the grated cheese evenly over the top of the potatoes. Place in the oven under the broiler at the LOW setting. You want to bring the dish back up to serving temperature and melt the cheese. Your goal? A pan of potatoes that looks gooey and bubbling with the cheese lightly browned on top.

7. Make sure you keep the pan low enough (NOT the top rack) so that the cheese doesn't immediately scorch. This dish needs only a few minutes for the cheese to melt and brown slightly, so watch it carefully! Once hot and bubbly, remove from broiler and serve immediately.

Glenn: *This old Spanish recipe for potatoes is good in the morning with breakfast eggs. We use a sweet smoked paprika from Spain (La Chinata is a good brand), which gives this dish an authentic flavor.*

Jorge: *If you have ever traveled in Spain, the smoked paprika is the spice that gives the markets such a distinctive aroma.*

Raúl: *You smell it everywhere!*

Jorge: *Papas Brava is also good as an accompaniment to any meat dish.*

Papas Brava
Spanish Potatoes

. . . .

INGREDIENTS

Serves 4 to 6

4 strips bacon, chopped

¼ cup olive oil for sautéing

½ cup chopped white onion

½ cup chopped green onions

½ cup chopped green bell pepper

4 cloves garlic, minced

3 cups washed and peeled, thinly sliced potatoes

Salt and freshly ground black pepper to taste

2 teaspoons sweet smoked paprika (Pimentón Dulce)

Chopped parsley for garnish

1. Sauté the bacon on low-medium heat in a large covered sauté pan until the fat is rendered. Add olive oil, onions, and bell pepper; continue sautéing until the onions get limp. Add the minced garlic and potatoes and toss to coat well. Lightly salt and pepper—you'll need to adjust the seasoning after the potatoes get tender so you can taste them.

2. Sprinkle on the paprika, cover, and cook at medium heat for 5 minutes. Reduce heat to low and let simmer. The dish is done when the potatoes are fork-tender, approximately 30 to 45 minutes. Sprinkle with chopped parsley and serve hot.

Plátanos Maduros
Fried Sweet Plantains

. . . .

INGREDIENTS

Serves 4

3 large very ripe plantains (heavy black spotting to a fully black skin)

   Corn oil, lard, or vegetable shortening

1. Peel and bias cut (diagonal) the plantain into 1-inch thick slices.

2. Heat your choice of oil until medium hot—a drop of water will sizzle. You need just enough oil to cover the bottom of the pan by a ½ inch or so. Sauté the pieces briefly at this high heat, about 1 minute per side.

3. Reduce heat to low and continue cooking uncovered, turning occasionally until they are brown and caramelized. Drain off excess oil and serve hot.

Variation: Some people like to lightly roll the plantains in white or brown sugar before frying.

Yuca con Ajo
Yuca with Garlic Sauce

. . . .

INGREDIENTS

Serves 6 to 8

1½	pounds yuca, peeled, halved and cut into chunks (frozen yuca may be available in Latin markets in your area)
1	teaspoon salt
	Juice of 1 lime
6	cloves garlic mashed into ½ teaspoon salt
⅓	cup lemon juice
1	onion, chopped fine
½	cup olive oil

1. Place yuca in a large 8-quart stockpot; add water until yuca is just covered. Add salt and lime juice, and bring to a boil. Reduce heat to low, cover, and simmer until tender—about 30 minutes. Drain. Remove any "woody" parts from center of yuca.

2. Mash garlic cloves into salt with a mortar and pestle. Add garlic, lemon juice, and onions to olive oil in a separate saucepan, heat until bubbling, then pour over yuca.

3. Toss the yuca and all ingredients lightly while continuing to sauté over medium heat until lightly browned but not crisp.

Glenn: *Yuca is another one of the root vegetables that are staples in Cuba.*

Jorge: *We especially like to eat it at parties and at holiday gatherings like Christmas Eve.*

Raúl: *Hey, when you make yuca, you need to remove any "woody" parts from the center of the yuca.*

Jorge: *Unless you like serving the "tooth pick" before the dessert tray, a major mistake in high-society dining!*

191

Jorge: *This is a great sauce to use with Tasajo, meat, fish—well, okay, just about everything.*

Raúl: Criolla *means "country style," and this simple sauce could easily be made in the country with ingredients that were commonly at hand.*

Glenn: *It's basically a variation of* sofrito, *the heart of so many Cuban dishes.*

Salsa Criolla
Creole Sauce
. . . .

INGREDIENTS

	Olive oil for sautéing
1	cup chopped onion
1	cup chopped green pepper
4	cloves garlic mashed with ½ teaspoon salt
5	fresh Roma tomatoes, peeled and chopped
1	(16-ounce) can tomato sauce
¼	teaspoon black pepper
1	teaspoon ground cumin
1	teaspoon oregano
1	tablespoon fresh lime juice
2	tablespoons red wine

1. Sauté the onion and green pepper until limp. Add the garlic/salt mixture and sauté an additional 1 or 2 minutes. Add the chopped tomatoes, tomato sauce, pepper, cumin, oregano, vinegar, and wine; bring to a boil, stirring constantly. Reduce heat to low and simmer, uncovered, for about 20 to 30 minutes, stirring occasionally. Serve as a sauce on your favorite dish.

192

Jorge: *Plantains are a staple in the Cuban diet. We use them in many different dishes, but you most frequently see them served as* maduros *(fried sweet plantains) and* tostones *(fried green plantain).*

Glenn: Tostones *are unique because they are fried twice. This double-frying technique is very popular in Cuba. Many cooks use it to make french-fried potatoes and* boniato *(sweet potato).*

Raúl: *The tradition of the* tostone *comes from African slaves. In the Congo, the people prepare plantains in exactly the same way, even to this day. It's another example of the culinary melting pot of Cuba.*

Tostones

Fried Green Plantain

. . . .

INGREDIENTS

Serves 4

Vegetable oil for frying

3 large green plantains, peeled and cut into 1-inch slices

Salt to taste

1. Fill a large skillet a third full with oil and heat over medium-high heat. Fry the plantain slices for approximately 3 to 5 minutes on each side, until they just begin to brown. Remove the plantain and drain on paper towels.

2. Use a plantain press or the bottom of a coffee cup to smash the plantains to about half their thickness.

3. Return the tostones to the pan and fry once again until golden brown on all sides. Remove and use paper towels to absorb excess oil. Sprinkle with salt to taste, and then serve.

TOCINILLO DE CIELO
Sit back, relax and have a
slice of Heavenly Custard
(recipe page 208).

Desserts

Arroz con Leche
Rice Pudding

. . . .

INGREDIENTS

Serves 4 to 6

½	cup uncooked white rice
1½	cups water
1	lemon rind
1	cinnamon stick
5	cups whole milk
¼	teaspoon salt
1	teaspoon vanilla extract
1¼	cup white cane sugar
	Cinnamon, ground

1. Cook the rice with water, lemon rind, and cinnamon stick until soft. Remove the lemon rind and cinnamon stick and drain off any excess water. (Most of the water should have been absorbed into the rice.)

2. Add milk, salt, vanilla extract, and sugar to rice and cook over low heat, uncovered, stirring occasionally until thick—about 45 minutes to 1 hour. As it thickens, stir more frequently to prevent burning!

3. Sprinkle with cinnamon and serve.

CUBAN DESSERTS

In Cuba, sugar cane is king and Cuban desserts tend to take advantage of the abundance of sugar. Cuban pastries are always very sweet and very rich. They are much sweeter than Mexican pastries, for example. Cuban desserts also feature many tropical flavors that are foreign to the American palate. By far, guava is the most popular fruit used in Cuban pastries and cakes. Cubans love to use it in everything! The signature pastry of Cuba is the pastelito. *It's a lot like the American turnover—a warm and flaky crust surrounding a sweet filling. However,* pastelito *fillings are typically Cuban. You're not going to be able to get these from Sara Lee (unless that's the name of the girl behind the counter at your local Cuban bakery)!*

Jorge: *On an island where sugar cane is the most important crop, it's no wonder that rum, the alcohol produced from sugar cane, finds its way into so many dishes. Rum gives recipes such a complex and interesting flavor!*

Raúl: *This recipe is so rich and moist, you won't believe it.*

Glenn: *Dieters beware! This is NOT a low-calorie dessert.*

Raúl: *Believe me, there's no such thing! Who ever heard of a diet dessert?*

Jorge: *If you slice the pieces small enough, all of the calories leak out …* (grin)

Cake de Ron
Rum Cake

. . . .

INGREDIENTS

Serves 12

3	cups flour
2	teaspoons baking powder
½	teaspoon baking soda
	Pinch of salt

1½	cups butter, softened
1½	cups granulated sugar
2	teaspoons pure vanilla extract
3	eggs plus 1 egg yolk
2	tablespoons grated lemon peel
½	cup dark rum
¼	cup banana liqueur
1	cup heavy whipping cream

Rum Syrup

5	ounces butter
¼	cup dark rum
¼	cup banana liqueur

(continued on page 202)

CAKE DE RON
A deliciously rich Rum Cake with Caramel Sauce (recipe page 203).

CUBAN
CAKES

CAKE IS NOT A historically Cuban dish. Early Cuban cake makers picked up most of their knowledge from the United States. In fact, the word torta, *used in many Latin countries for the word* cake, *is not used in Cuba. In Cuban Spanish, the word is* cake, *directly assimilated from English. It is often given a Cuban pronunciation: Ka-Kay.*

Cake de Ron (continuation)

Rum Cake

. . . .

¾   cup white sugar

Powdered sugar for dusting

1. Preheat oven to 350 degrees F.

2. To make the cake, sift flour, baking powder, baking soda, and salt; set aside.

3. With an electric mixer, cream together the butter and sugar. Add vanilla and eggs and beat until blended. Beat in the lemon peel and then add the rum and banana liqueurs. Gradually add the flour, alternating with the cream. Blend mixture until just combined. Pour batter into a well-greased and floured Bundt (circular ring) pan and bake approximately 1 hour. A skewer inserted in the cake should come out clean.

4. To make the syrup, melt the butter in a 2-quart saucepan. Add rum, banana liqueur, and sugar. Slowly bring to a rolling boil, reduce heat to medium and cook until it reduces somewhat, about 10 to 15 minutes. Do not overcook. Let cool.

5. Remove the cake from the oven and place it on a cooling rack. Use a skewer and poke holes all over the cake. Spoon the syrup evenly over the cake. Let stand for 30 minutes, so that the syrup soaks in.

6. Finally, carefully turn the cake over onto a serving plate. Dust with powdered sugar.

Dulce de Leche Salsa

Caramel Sauce

. . . .

INGREDIENTS

1	cup sugar
½	cup water
3	tablespoons light corn syrup
8	tablespoons butter
1¼	cup heavy cream

1. Bring the sugar, water, and corn syrup to a rolling boil in a 3-quart saucepan, stirring constantly on high heat until the sugar begins to caramelize and turn lightly golden, about 4 to 5 minutes. A lot of the water will boil off at this point.

2. Quickly whisk in 6 tablespoons butter, and continue cooking, stirring constantly, for about 2 to 3 minutes. Whisk in 1 cup of the cream and continue cooking on medium-high heat, stirring constantly, until the mixture starts to turn golden brown and thicken—about 4 to 5 minutes. Remove from heat, stir in 2 tablespoons of butter and ¼ cup heavy cream. Continue stirring a minute or two to prevent any scorching.

3. Let cool, use immediately warm or refrigerate for later. Just heat slightly in the microwave to make it easier to pour.

Jorge: *This sauce is delicious on several desserts, including ice cream.*

Glenn: *We've used it on both flan and cheesecake.*

Jorge: *Drizzle this sauce over a simple cake or pudding and you'll have a one-minute masterpiece . . .*

Glenn: *. . . what the TV chefs call "good presentation!"*

Jorge: *Flan is such a wonderfully rich dessert, creamy and full of egg flavor like a very rich custard.*

Glenn: *However, it's very easy to make. In fact, we have simplified this recipe over the years to make it as easy as possible.*

Jorge: *Even a ten-year-old can do a good job with this recipe!*

Raúl: *So if you're having trouble, run out and find a ten-year-old!*

Jorge: *No, really, your guests will think you worked all afternoon on this delicious treat.*

Glenn: *The only tricky part is melting the sugar. Many recipes suggest adding water to the sugar, but this is not really necessary.*

Jorge: *Okay, if you want to wimp out and play it safe, add a tablespoon of water. But believe us, there's plenty of water in that "dry" sugar!*

Flan

Cuban Custard

. . . .

INGREDIENTS

Serves 8

	Rind of 1 lemon, carefully pared
1½	cups milk
1	cinnamon stick
¾	cup sugar
4	whole eggs
4	egg yolks
¾	cup sugar
1½	cups heavy cream

1. Preheat oven to 350 degrees F.

2. Use a soufflé or baking dish with a 5-cup capacity. You can also use individual ovenproof custard cups.

3. Carefully remove the outer rind from a lemon. Don't cut too deep or you'll cut into the pulp. You just want the outer, mostly yellow layer.

4. Scald the milk by bringing it quickly to a boil with the lemon rind and cinnamon stick, stirring constantly. Remove from heat and let stand for 15 minutes. Remove lemon rind and cinnamon stick after the milk cools.

5. For the caramel, heat ¾ cup sugar in the bottom of a metallic pan at medium-high heat until it begins to melt. Stir constantly to prevent burning! The sugar will turn to a thick syrup with a light brown color. Quickly remove from heat and pour into a flan dish or into each one of your individual custard cups. Tilt back and forth to cover the bottom and sides of the dish. The syrup will harden fast as it cools to form a thick shell. During the baking process, this shell magically transforms itself into a delicious dark caramel syrup.

6. For the custard, beat the eggs and egg yolks with ¾ cup sugar until thoroughly mixed and slightly frothy; stir in the warm milk and the cream. Strain the mixture through a sieve (straining will result in a smoother flan), pour into the caramel-lined dish(es) and set it into a water bath (*baño de Maria*) with about an inch of water in the bottom.

7. Bake for 40 to 50 minutes (reduce time if you use shallower or individual dishes) or until a knife inserted in the center comes out clean. Let cool in dish.

8. Before serving, loosen sides with a knife and flip onto a platter with a rim. Be sure to spoon plenty of the syrup over each serving. If using individual custard cups, just let the flan cool, sprinkle with a little cinnamon for color, and serve in the cup.

Jorge: *When was the last time you had some comfort food? You know, one of those home-cooked specialties that brings back memories of your childhood?*

Glenn: *At my house, that would have been macaroni and cheese and fried hot dogs.*

Raúl: *Not exactly comfort food!*

Jorge: *When I was growing up in Bauta, every Cuban family enjoyed this delicious treat.*

Raúl: *It's a Cuban version of pudding. It's not fancy, it's not hard to make, but one taste brings back some wonderful memories of Cuba.*

Glenn: *To Cuba! To old memories and memories yet to come.*

Natilla

Cuban Pudding

INGREDIENTS

Serves 8

1	quart milk
¼	teaspoon salt
1	piece of lime rind
1	cinnamon stick
8	egg yolks
1½	cups light brown sugar
⅓	cup cornstarch
½	cup water
2	teaspoons vanilla
1	teaspoon cinnamon (optional)
	Grated coconut (optional)
	Nutmeg and/or cinnamon for dusting

1. Pour the milk into a 4-quart saucepan. Add salt, lime rind, and cinnamon stick, and bring to a boil. Reduce heat to low and simmer for about 10 minutes, stirring occasionally. Let cool. Remove cinnamon and lime peel.

2. Beat egg yolks with an electric mixer until fluffy. Continue beating and gradually add sugar until creamy. Gradually add milk until smooth. Place the mixture in the top half of a double boiler over high heat and begin to cook, stirring occasionally until it's bubbling hot.

3. Mix cornstarch with water and add to the mixture, stirring constantly until it thickens. Add more cornstarch mixed with water as needed to achieve a thick pudding-like consistency.

4. To bring back those pleasant memories of warm tropical girls and cool Havana nights, stir in a teaspoon of ground cinnamon and a handful of grated coconut after the mixture thickens. Cook for an additional 5 minutes, stirring constantly.

5. Remove from heat and stir in vanilla. Pour into individual serving bowls or custard cups. Chill completely in refrigerator. Sprinkle nutmeg or cinnamon on top just before serving.

Glenn: *Tocinillo de Cielo is a distant cousin of flan. It is sometimes mistakenly called* tocino del cielo, *which literally means "bacon from heaven."*

Jorge: *It doesn't look like bacon, it doesn't taste like bacon—in fact, there's no bacon in it.*

Raúl: *So why people started calling it this, we'll never know.*

Jorge: *No matter what you call it,* Tocinillo de Cielo *is sweeter and lighter than flan, light on the tongue— you'll find yourself tempted to inhale this stuff!*

Raúl: *There are two types: one has a slight lemon taste and the other tastes like almonds. This is the recipe for the lemon one. To add an almond flavor, use the variation at the end of the recipe.*

Tocinillo de Cielo
Heavenly Custard

. . . .

INGREDIENTS

Serves 8

¾	cup white sugar
1½	cups white sugar
2	cups water
	Peel of 1 medium lemon
14	egg yolks
2	teaspoons pure vanilla extract
2	teaspoons grated lemon peel

1. Preheat oven to 350 degrees F.

2. Use a soufflé or baking dish, about 5-cup capacity. You can also use individual ovenproof custard cups.

3. For the caramel, heat ¾ cup sugar in the bottom of a metallic pan at medium-high heat until it begins to melt. Stir constantly to prevent burning.

4. The sugar will turn to a thick syrup with a light brown color. Quickly remove from heat and pour into your flan dish or into the individual custard cups. Tilt back and forth to cover the bottom and sides of the dish. The syrup will harden fast as it cools to form a thick shell. During the baking process, this shell magically transforms itself into a delicious dark caramel syrup.

5. For the tocinillo, combine 1½ cups sugar with water in a 3-quart saucepan. Add lemon peel and boil at high heat, stirring occasionally, until the syrup reaches a temperature of exactly 220 degrees F. Remove from heat immediately. Remove lemon peel. Let cool until moderately warm. We use the Raúl "single digit" method. We stick one of Raúl's fingers in the syrup and if he doesn't yell, it's ready …

6. Beat egg yolks by hand with a whisk until slightly frothy. Blend in vanilla and grated lemon peel. Gradually add the moderately warm syrup. Blend to a smooth consistency.

7. Strain the mixture through a sieve (straining through a sieve will result in a smoother tocinillo), and pour into the caramelized baking dish or individual custard cups.

8. Next, place the baking dish or custard cups in a water bath (*baño de Maria*) with about 1 inch of water in the bottom.

9. Bake in the oven for 45 minutes to 1 hour. To check for doneness, poke a toothpick or fork in it while baking; it should come out relatively clean. If you are using individual custard cups, check after 30 minutes.

10. After the tocinillo is fully cooked, set aside and let cool.

11. When ready to serve, run a knife along the edge to loosen it. Place a serving platter over the bowl or pan and flip it quickly. Make sure to scrape as much caramel from the bowl as you can onto the tocinillo (that's the best part). Or serve in the individual custard cups.

Variation:

Omit the lemon peel. Add 2 tablespoons Amaretto liqueur.

Tres Leches Cake

Three Milks Cake

· · · · · · · · · · · · · · · · · · · ·

INGREDIENTS

Serves 12

Cake

2	cups cake flour
2	teaspoons baking powder
½	teaspoon salt
6	large eggs, separated
2	cups granulated sugar
2	teaspoons vanilla extract
½	cup whole milk

Syrup

1	(14-ounce) can sweetened condensed milk
1	(14-ounce) can evaporated milk
1¼	cups heavy cream
2	tablespoons light rum (a little more if you are in a party mood!)

Frosting

4	egg whites
½	teaspoon cream of tartar
½	cup water
1½	cups sugar
1	cup light corn syrup

Raúl: *This is one of the most delicious cakes ever invented. It's really a Nicaraguan dessert …*

Jorge: *… but it is served in just about every Cuban restaurant in Miami.*

Glenn: *It is a very rich and filling cake. It gets its name from the three milks—sweetened condensed milk, evaporated milk, and heavy cream—that are soaked into the cake, making it the moistest and most delicious cake you've ever had.*

Jorge: *The cake is like one big giant sponge soaking up the delicious milk syrup.*

Raúl: *You can actually eat this one with a spoon!*

210

1. Preheat oven to 350 degrees F. Grease and lightly flour a 9 x 13-inch baking dish.

2. To prepare the cake, sift together the flour, baking powder, and salt.

3. Separate the egg yolks and whites. Beat the whites until very foamy and frothy. Set aside. In a large mixing bowl, cream the sugar, egg yolks, and vanilla extract with an electric mixer. As you continue mixing, slowly add the milk. Then add the flour mixture, a little at a time, until all the flour is incorporated and the batter is smooth. Finally, use a spatula to gently fold in the beaten egg whites until completely mixed.

4. Pour batter into the baking dish. Bake for 35 to 45 minutes, or until a toothpick stuck in the middle comes out clean. Remove from oven and allow cake to cool on a wire rack for 20 minutes. Now it's time to get fancy. Invert the cake onto a jelly roll pan or a baking tray with a raised edge on it— something to catch the syrup! Use a fork to repeatedly pierce the top of the cake.

5. For the milk syrup, whisk together the sweetened condensed milk, evaporated milk, heavy cream, and rum in a mixing bowl, until well blended. Slowly pour syrup over the cake a little at a time and let it soak in. Be patient! Use your fork to help it along a bit, piercing here and there through the syrup until most of the milk syrup is absorbed. Don't worry if there is still a pool of syrup around the bottom of the cake, it will gradually soak in.

6. Cover the syrup-drenched cake in plastic wrap and refrigerate for at least 3 hours before frosting.

7. For the frosting, beat the egg whites with the cream of tartar in a large bowl until they form stiff peaks. Set aside. In a separate pan, mix the water, sugar, and corn syrup. Cook over high heat, stirring constantly, until a candy thermometer reads 230 degrees F. Remove from heat. While beating the egg whites with an electric mixer, pour the hot syrup into the egg whites all at once; continue beating for about 5 minutes. With the addition of the hot syrup, your frosting should "puff up" and thicken. Let the frosting cool at room temperature. Use a wet spatula to spread a thick layer of the frosting on the top and sides of the cake.

8. To serve, cut individual squares, top with a red maraschino cherry, and serve cold.

(continued on next page)

211

Tres Leches Cake (continuation)
Three Milks Cake

· ·

Variations:

Banana Tres Leches Cake

Add ⅓ cup banana liqueur to the milk syrup, omit rum, and reduce the evaporated milk to ¾ can.

Cuatro Leches Cake

Many Miami restaurants now serve a Cuatro Leches Cake. This is the basic Tres Leches Cake with a topping of Dulce de Leche (caramel sauce). If you want to serve this, follow recipe instructions above. Serve the cake in a bowl or round sundae dish. Add a layer of Dulce de Leche (page 202) around the sides of the cake in the bowl.

Cuban Food Glossary

Cuban Food Glossary

. . . .

A la Parrilla—means that the food—usually meats and seafood—is grilled or barbecued.

Aquacate—is an avocado. It is popular in salads or eaten plain, although there is no such thing as Cuban guacamole!

Arepa—comes from Colombia and is a type of grilled cheese sandwich. Instead of bread, *arepas* are slightly sweet corn pancakes, fried on a griddle with a thin layer of Swiss cheese between the two cakes. These are normally eaten by hand, just like a sandwich.

Arroz con Pollo—is a Cuban Sunday-lunch favorite. It's chicken and rice, a dish whose cousin is familiar to most Americans. Whether seasoned with saffron strands or colored with Bijol, the rice is bright yellow with tender pieces of chicken. Wine, olive oil, and spices give it a wonderful aroma and delicious flavor.

Arroz con Leche—is rice pudding. This dessert is very sweet and creamy with a great taste of cinnamon. It sometimes includes raisins and is many times flavored with good Cuban rum.

Baño de Maria—is the Spanish name for "water bath," basically a pan of water that goes in the oven. When making flan, you place the flan mixture into custard cups or a baking dish and then set these in the baño de Maria. The water bath prevents the bottom of the flan from burning. We usually use a 6 x 9-inch metal cake pan with an inch or two of water as a Baño de Maria. However, you can use anything that holds water and can go in the oven! Tip: If you are using individual custard cups, place a clean dish towel in the bottom of your Baño de Maria. This will keep the cups from sliding around on the trip into and out of the oven!

Bollitos—are fried nuggets made with ground black-eyed peas.

Boliche—is Cuban pot roast. A slit is made in a beef roast and it is stuffed with chorizo and usually onions, green pepper, garlic, and spices. Sometimes ham is used in place of the chorizo. The chorizo and ham give the beef a smoky flavor.

Bijol—is a powder made with annatto seeds. It is used instead of saffron for coloring rice in many recipes, mainly because saffron is expensive. Bijol does not really duplicate the saffron flavor; however, it does have a flavor all its own that is unmistakable in Cuban dishes. You also might see Bijol sold as Badia Yellow Coloring.

Boniato—is a Cuban sweet potato that is drier than, and not as sweet as, the common American varieties. In flavor boniato is a cross between a sweet and a baking potato, with a fluffier texture and a very mild taste.

Café Cubano—is espresso coffee Cuban-style. Very strong, very black, and very sweet, it's served in a tiny cup. High in caffeine, Cuban coffee will really give you a jolt.

Café con Leche—is a Cuban coffee with milk. Your order includes a cup of steamed milk and a Cuban coffee; pour the coffee into the milk and drink. Add more sugar if you need to. It's a good way for non-Cubans to acquire a taste for Cuban coffee.

Calabaza—is a type of pumpkin used in cooking. Its flavor is closer to squash than to pumpkin. The color of the skin ranges from green to light reddish orange. The meat of the calabaza is orange. Just about every Latin and Mexican market we've gone to stocks calabaza in season. If it's not available in your area, you may substitute butternut squash in most recipes.

Chimichurri—is the green sauce you see served with many beef dishes and sometimes as a dipping sauce for Cuban bread. It's made with garlic, parsley or cilantro, vinegar or lime juice, and olive oil.

Chorizo—is a type of sausage. The Cuban variety is not hot and spicy like its Mexican cousin. It is a dry, hard sausage heavily flavored with garlic and paprika. A good chorizo is the essential building block of an excellent paella.

Churrasco—is a long flat cut of skirt steak. It's typically marinated to make it tender and full of flavor. It's always served with a good *chimichurri* sauce. In Argentina, where this style of cooking developed, *churrasco* actually refers to many types of meats prepared over an open fire. In Miami, *churrasco* specifically refers to a cut of beef prepared in the Argentine style.

Cilantro and **Culantro**—are two plants that look different but taste a lot alike. Cilantro has a sharper bite than its cousin, culantro, which has a somewhat musty flavor. Both herbs were used in Cuba. In fact, culantro grew wild all over the island. Many Cuban cooks prefer to use culantro for its subtly different flavor.

Congri—Please don't confuse this dish, as many do, with Moros y Cristianos. The dishes are similar in that the beans are cooked with the rice. The traditional Congri of Cuba Oriente is made with red beans instead of black.

Cortadito—is half Cuban coffee and half hot milk.

Croquetas—have a filling of ground ham or other meat with a light batter. These delicious little snacks are deep fried until golden brown. On the appetizer menu in many restaurants, they are a favorite walk-away item at bakeries and lunch counters.

Cuatro Leches—Many Miami restaurants now serve a *cuatro leches* cake. This is the basic *tres leches* cake with a toping of *dulce de leche,* a caramel sauce.

Cuban Sandwich—is a delicious combination of ham, Cuban roast pork, Swiss cheese, and dill pickles served on half a loaf of fresh Cuban bread. The sandwich is heated and pressed flat in a sandwich press, or *plancha.* This melts the cheese and crisps the crust. Most restaurants offer a "regular" Cuban sandwich and a "special." What's so special about it? Well, guess which one includes more meat?

Empanadas—are fluffy turnovers filled with ham, beef, picadillo, cheese, or other ingredients.

Enchilado—is a delicious stew. Some of the best are made with fish and seafood. See "Tortillas" for more information.

Ensalada de Aguacate—is an avocado salad, sometimes served halved and stuffed with shrimp, chicken, or tuna salad.

Flan—is a rich egg custard. Flan is poured into a pan with a coating of dark caramelized sugar. Once baked in the oven, the caramel liquifies to create a delicious thin syrup. For a real treat, serve it topped with sweetened shredded coconut. Yum!

Frijoles Negros—are black beans in a thick gravy with garlic, onion, green pepper, and spices. It's the signature dish of Cuba, eaten at just about every meal and usually served over rice as a side dish.

Frita—No, it's not a corn chip! It's a Cuban hamburger. The Havana-style concoction includes ground beef, ground pork, and several secret spices, depending on where you get one. *Frita* also means "fried." So *yuca frita* is fried yuca (like a French fry) and *vaca frita* is fried cow (how do they find a frying pan big enough?)

Frituras, or Frituritas—are what Americans would call fritters. Cuban *frituras* are made from dough that may include several root vegetables, such as malanga or boniato. They may contain fish or meat with onions, garlic, peppers, and other spices.

Fruta Bomba—is what Americans call papaya. However, if you're in Miami, or in a Cuban restaurant or market, or anywhere with Cubans around, always ask for *fruta bomba,* not papaya. You'll save yourself a lot of embarrassment. Why? Let's just say that papaya has a slang meaning to ALL Cubans. That's all we can say here because this is a family-friendly cookbook.

Fufú or Fufú de Plátanos Verdes—is a delicious dish similar to mashed potatoes. *Fufú* has a delicious garlic flavor with a hint of lemon or lime. What really makes it sing are the delicious pieces of roast pork that are mashed into the plantain.

Guayaba—is guava, used as a filling in cakes and pastries.

Lechón Asado—is Cuban pork roast, whether a roast, a fresh ham, or a whole pig. The pork is marinated overnight in mojo marinade: sour orange, loads of garlic, and spices.

Lechuga y Tomate—is lettuce and tomato, as in salad. This is a simple dinner salad served with oil-and-vinegar dressing.

Maduros, or Plátanos Maduros—is sweet plantain, sliced diagonally and sautéed. Plantains need to be very ripe, almost black, before cooking. They are very sweet with a strong banana-and-caramelized-sugar flavor. Many non-Cubans turn up their noses at them. ("Fried bananas?") Try them. Then try them again. You'll love them!

Malanga—is another root vegetable that is popular with Cubans. It comes in both white and yellow varieties. Malanga is very easily digested and is often used as a baby food. It is very closely related to the taro root. Malanga is also often made into flour and used in cakes, breads, and pastries. Malanga flour is a great substitute for cornstarch to thicken or "tighten up" stews and sauces, and malanga fritters are very popular. Malanga is sold in most Latin and Mexican groceries.

Mariquitas—are plantain, yuca, or casava chips that are sliced extremely thin and deep fried. You can find them in bags in supermarkets. The best ones are at restaurants and lunch counters, made fresh and served hot with a splash of mojo.

Mariscos—are seafood, so *arroz con mariscos* is simply "seafood with rice." Mariscos usually include shrimp, scallops, lobster, fish, clams, mussels, and so on.

Masa Flour (Masa Harina)—is a corn flour used to make tamales and as a thickening agent in many dishes.

Masitas de Puerco Fritas—are fried pork chunks seasoned to perfection with mojo marinade and usually served with onions.

Medianoche, or Midnight Sandwich—is the Cuban sandwich's sweeter cousin, so named because it is a great treat for after a movie or a night of dancing. It has the same ingredients as a Cuban sandwich, it gets the same treatment in the sandwich press, but it's made with sweeter, lighter egg bread.

Mojo (Mojito)—is used as a marinade and sauce. It's made with sour orange juice, loads of garlic, onions, and spices.

Moros y Cristianos—are similar to *frijoles negros,* but the beans are cooked together with the rice.

Palomilla—is a thinly sliced (sometimes pounded thin) steak. It's cooked with lime juice, garlic, and onions, and is sometimes served with *chimichurri.*

Pan con Bistec—is a Cuban steak sandwich. The steak is very thin and prepared like a palomilla steak with lime juice, garlic, and onions. Many places serve it with crispy shoestring potatoes on top of the meat.

Pan Cubano—is Cuban bread.

Papá Rellenas—are balls made with mashed potatoes and stuffed with picadillo or seasoned beef. These delicate little morsels are deep fried and taste wonderful.

Papás Fritas—are French fries. Just like the American version in most respects, except a lot of Cuban-style fries are sliced very thin—like shoestring potatoes.

Parboiled rice—is made by soaking, steaming, and drying rice before it goes through the milling process. The most popular parboiled rice in the United States is Uncle Ben's Converted Rice. There are also many Latin food companies that sell their own brand of parboiled rice. For years, chefs looked down their noses at parboiled rice, but in recent years, even gourmet chefs have developed an appreciation for this rice, because it cooks up fluffy and separate. Contrary to popular belief, the parboiling process actually drives the nutrients into the rice grain, making parboiled rice more nutritious than standard white rice.

Pasta de Guayaba—is guava paste, or *dulce de guayaba*. You'll see it in supermarkets in big cans. Use it on toast, or the more traditional favorite is to have a slice of guava paste on a cracker with cream cheese or farmer cheese. Caution, the Cuban version of farmer cheese is very sharp and salty!

Picadillo—is Cuban-style hash (some call it the Cuban Sloppy Joe) and a favorite meal of most Cubans. It's ground beef with tomato, green pepper, green olives, or capers and, of course, plenty of garlic. It's frequently served over rice with tostones.

Rabo Encendido—is oxtail stew. In America, oxtails actually come from a cow. Oxtail is skinned and usually sold cut into pieces. Obviously, the tail of a cow has a lot of bone! However, the meat, when slow cooked, is very tender and delicious!

Ron—is rum, and Cuba has been famous throughout its history for rum. However, there are only two authentic and delicious Cuban rums being made today and neither one is made in Cuba: they are Bacardi and Matusalem. The

Bacardi family began making rum in Santiago de Cuba in 1862. They were the first company to "civilize" this crudely made drink, long favored by pirates and seamen. Matusalem entered the business in 1872 and developed a highly refined product known as the Cognac of Rums. If you want real Cuban rum, pick either Bacardi or Matusalem!

Ropa Vieja—is shredded beef in a type of stew with tomatoes, onions, garlic, and green pepper.

Sopa de Plátanos—is plantain soup. If you like chicken noodle soup, we guarantee that you'll love this soup.

Tamales—are not very much like the Mexican version; Cuban tamales are not spicy hot, and the meat is mixed in with the dough. If you order just one, it's called a *tamal*—never a tamale. *Tamales* is the plural form of *tamal.* That's one of the reasons why Glenn always asks for two!

Tasajo—is dried beef that's been reconstituted. It can be used in a stew with tomatoes and spices, or served fried. A real traditional Cuban comfort food!

Tocinillo del Cielo—is a distant cousin to flan. It's sweeter and lighter than flan, light on the tongue—you'll find yourself tempted to inhale this stuff! There are two common types: one has a slight lemon-citrus taste and the other tastes like almonds.

Tortilla—is a Cuban egg dish similar to an omelet or frittata; it usually includes potatoes and onions. However, there are many variations, including some with ham, cheese, chorizo, rice, and ripe plantain—even shrimp! See "Enchilado" for more information.

Tostones—are thick slices of plantain, fried, flattened, and fried again, then served hot and salted.

Tres Leches Cake—is really a Nicaraguan dessert, but it is served in just about every Cuban restaurant in Miami. The "three milks" name comes from the mixture—sweetened condensed milk, evaporated milk, and heavy cream—that is poured over the cake in mass quantities until it is dripping. The whole thing is topped with a meringue frosting and a bright red cherry!

Turrones—are almond candies imported from Spain and a traditional holiday treat. They come in several flavors, including chocolate, nougat, honey, fruit, and egg.

Vaca Frita—literally means "fried cow." (And you thought your Spanish/English Palm Pilot had gone crazy!) It is a beef roast that is slow roasted or simmered until the meat is soft and stringy. It is then sautéed with onions, garlic, green pepper, and spices.

Yuca—is another one of the root vegetables that are staples in Cuba. The most common preparation is with lemon, garlic, and olive oil—a great side dish! Most Americans have eaten yuca without even knowing it. Have you ever had tapioca? All tapioca products are derived from yuca! Yuca flour is also used in cooking, especially as a thickening agent.

Sources

. . . .

TWENTY YEARS AGO you couldn't find many Latin ingredients anywhere outside of the major cities. Finding typical Cuban ingredients was even more difficult! With more interest in Latin cooking and an ever-increasing Latin population, many of these previously unheard-of ingredients can now be found at your local grocer—even in Cleveland or Des Moines! In addition, many cities, both large and small, now have Latin and ethnic markets. You may have to seek out these little places in a likely looking neighborhood near you. The small "mom and pop" shops often carry the full range of items that are essential to the Cuban kitchen. These include tropical fruits like mangoes, guava, and papaya; root vegetables like yuca, malanga, and boniato; and of course, the ever-popular plantain!

We realize that you may be somewhere where you just can't find the ingredients you need. For those of you so unlucky that your community remains untouched by Latin culture, we have provided this list of Latin food sources.

Tienda.com Fine Products from Spain

This Internet-based store is a great source for Spanish chorizo, morcilla, Serrano ham, cheeses, olive oil, smoked paprika (Pimentón), spices, sidra, and a nice selection of Spanish wines.

Tienda.com
3701 Rochambeau Road
Williamsburg VA 23188
757.566.9606

888.472.1022 toll free
757.566.9603 fax
www.tienda.com

El Latinazo

This is another Internet-based store with a good selection of exotic tropical fruits (mostly frozen fruit pulps), root vegetables, and spices.

El Latinazo
www.ellatinazo.com

Cuban Food Market

Everything for the Cuban chef. If you can't find it here, it's probably not available on the Internet! Items include the hard-to-find Bijol powder, a full range of spices, Sazón Goya or Sazón Tropical, guava pastes and jellies, sour orange juice (naranja agria), prepared mojo marinades, beans, fruits, and vegetables. It's the only place online that we know of where you can get real cachucha peppers!

Cuban Food Market
3100 SW 8th Street
Miami FL 33135
877.999.9945 toll free
305.644.8861 fax
www.cubanfoodmarket.com

About the Three Guys From Miami

. . . .

THE THREE GUYS FROM MIAMI are brothers-in-law. Brought together by fate, they became fast friends who share a passion for good food, good conversation, and a great party. Together they run one of the most popular Web sites dedicated to Cuban culture on the Internet: "iCuban.com: The Internet Cuban" made its debut in 1996 and has continued to grow in size and popularity each year. More than 3 million people have visited the Three Guys on the World Wide Web.

The Three Guys' own history predates the Web. Jorge and Glenn met in 1981, and once Glenn met Raúl in 1983 the guys immediately became a team. For the past twenty years they have been perfecting their Cuban recipes by cooking, and eating—oh yes, a LOT of eating—Cuban food. They have made several appearances on the Food Network and are frequent sources of Cuban cooking tips and advice for professional and amateur chefs all over the world.

Raúl Musibay

BORN IN CAYO LA ROSA, near Bauta, in the province of Havana, Raúl brought his family to the United States via Spain in 1980. Except for one winter spent in New Jersey, Raúl has been a full-time Miami resident ever since. He reports, "Man, it was just too cold there!" Raúl is known in Miami for his love of fishing, his great parties, and his mastery of the Cuban pig roast. When not roasting a pig or planning his next social gathering, Raúl is the manager of the Red Bird Amoco station in Miami. He arrived in the U. S. knowing very little English. On his first day on the job his manager told him to answer the phone. Raúl said, "What if there is an American guy calling?" And his manager said, "Well you better get used to it, Raúl. There are a lot of American guys here in the United States!" Raúl and his wife, Esther, have two married children, Onel (a detective with the Miami-Dade police force) and Onix (a mechanical engineer who also lives in Miami). Two grandchildren, Gabriel and Madison, Raúl's mother, Amparo, and mother-in-law, Georgina, make up the rest of his extended family.

Glenn Lindgren

NO, HE'S NOT Cuban, he doesn't speak Spanish (at least not very well) and technically, he isn't even from Miami—but he sure spends a lot of time here! Glenn grew up in Minneapolis and first came to Miami in 1984 where he fell in love with the city, the people, and Cuban culture. He says the nice thing about Miami is that just about everyone is from somewhere else. "I have two hometowns: the one I grew up in and my adopted hometown of Miami," Glenn says. "I spend as much time as I can in Miami, especially during those cold Minnesota winters. A freelance writer by profession, Glenn has made it his life's work to document the antics of the Three Guys from Miami, both in books and on the Internet. Glenn has spent twenty-four years learning about Cuban culture and Cuban food. "I found out early on that if I wanted to eat Cuban food in Minnesota, I'd have to learn to cook it myself," he says. When not in Miami, Glenn and his wife, Maureen, live in the frozen northland of Minnesota with two daughters, Erin and Gabrielle, and a son, Dennis. Most of the year you can find him there dreaming about warm ocean breezes and hot Cuban sandwiches!

Jorge Castillo

JORGE IS A proud Marielito, one of the thousands of honest, hard-working Cubans who came to the United States via the Mariel Boatlift in 1980. Also born and raised in Cayo la Rosa, Jorge left Miami after three months to live in Iowa, where he hoped to learn to speak English and expose himself to American culture in the heartland. "Living in Iowa for eighteen years gave me an appreciation for other Cubans who live far away from Cuban culture centers," Jorge says. He was frequently homesick for his favorite Cuban foods. "You just can't get a loaf of Cuban bread anywhere in Iowa!" During the Iowa years, Jorge and Glenn became frequent collaborators on Cuban feasts prepared for family and friends. "We introduced a lot of Iowans to the Cuban pig roast," Jorge adds. However, with plenty of ties to Miami, it was inevitable that Jorge would one day return. He is now the regional sales manager for a major medical products company. He and his wife, Mary, and their two daughters, Mariel and Allison, make their home in Miami's West Dade.

Index